*

Let Me Survive

*

Let Me Survive

A TRUE STORY

Louise Longo

with Marie-Thérèse Cuny

Translated by Alison Anderson

SHERIDAN HOUSE

Published 1996 by
Sheridan House, Inc.
145 Palisade Street
Dobbs Ferry, NY 10522

Cataloging-In-Publication Data

Longo, Louise.
  [Elle dort dans la mer, English]
  Let me survive: a true story / Louise Longo with
Marie-Thérèse Cuny; translated by Alison Anderson.
    p. cm.
  ISBN 1-57409-006-2 (alk. paper)
  1. Jan Van Gent (Ketch) 2. Longo, Louise.
  3. Survival after airplane accidents, shipwrecks, etc.
  I. Cuny, Marie-Thérèse. II. Title.
  G530.J34L6613 1996
  910.4'5--dc20   96-8897
                                         CIP

Editor: Janine Simon
Designer: Jeremiah B. Lighter

Printed in the United States of America

ISBN 1-57409-006-2

For Bernard and Gaëlla

For Marie

For my family

and all the unknown people
who helped me so greatly.

To Win

If you think you are defeated, then you are.
If you think you won't dare, then you won't.
If you like to win but think that you cannot,
Your defeat is almost certain.
If you think you shall lose, then you are lost,
For success begins with wanting.
It is all a question of your state of mind.
Life's battles are not always won
By the strongest or the quickest of men.
But sooner or later the man who wins
Is he who thinks that he can.

FRANK MICHAËL

The sea is the most beautiful gift of nature, and
the only place where one is master after God,
because the punishment of the sin committed
needs no tribunal to be judged.

CLAUDE HARLÉ

Contents

CHAPTER ONE

The Next Day I Was Smiling

I STAND ACCUSED.

The courtroom is huge, and a lot of people have gathered here.

"You never leave a boat as long as it is afloat. Those people were foolish."

"Adrift for two weeks on the open ocean without food? Impossible, she'd be in worse shape than that."

"There's something not quite right about it. She's the only survivor; that's odd."

"And what if it were a voluntary disappearance?"

"She killed her husband!"

"She drowned her daughter!"

"If the French police are looking for her, there must be something to it . . ."

"The next day she was smiling!"

Perhaps that is the sentence which hurt me the most. Everyone was talking about me, writing about me, taking my picture, questioning me, and I no longer knew where I stood. The land for which I had hoped so intensely, for which I had prayed, whose help I wanted so badly, was throwing me back into the ocean. Guilty. I tried to give them an answer:

"I drank rain water . . ."

What I read, in their movie cameras, in their lenses, was that I should have died. Even better, I should have died before their eyes and, in trying to rescue me, they would have had to tear me from the decomposing bodies of my husband and daughter. And in a last sigh of exhaustion I would have murmured:

"Give them a decent burial . . ."

I would have died right there before their cameras. No more smiles for the next day.

I would have given the media and a public greedy for other people's tragedies the same image as that of the small girl who slowly drowned in the mud before a reporter's telephoto lens. Then the headlines and editorials could have competed for the best story about little me. Woman of courage, mother courage. They could have told a story without knowing any of the true story; they could have embroidered and imagined things. My mother would have wept on our graves, and the god of public opinion would have forgiven me.

Instead, I had gotten it all wrong, as they say at school. The merry widow, said a few vitriolic lines; I was already under suspicion in less time than it takes to make an investigation. I was "questionable," in any case, and above all at a distance.

It has been more than a year now since a Spanish helicopter picked me up from a liferaft, alone, after fifteen days of drifting. Well, you know what? I didn't tell the truth then.

I did lie, that's true.

Here is the truth. And tell the truth I will, without superlatives and fancy phrases. Because I am neither a writer nor a journalist. Because I am an ordinary woman, victim of something much larger than myself, and I use simple words. And so that they leave me alone, once and for all. A book is still much better at telling the truth than a three-minute interview, a photo snapped in a crowd, a consul's suspicions, and a policeman's interrogation.

Once the book is finished I'll be able to tell those who still feel like asking questions:

"Read it. That's what it's for. And now let me survive."

CHAPTER TWO

Casting Off

B ERNARD. I had difficulty recognizing him. A four- or five-day beard, tousled hair, a wrinkled shirt, African trousers and thong sandals. Not a good impression.

At the age of fifty Bernard looks like a tired adventurer. Since we separated two years ago, life has not been kind to him.

When I'm around him I am always torn between a feeling of maternal protectiveness and a woman's irritation. I am also pretty sure that if I'm not there by his side he'll be badly organized, live any old way, eat any old thing and just basically lose control. I wonder if all ex-wives are like me, preserving a tenderness for the man they once loved, and this very fraternal friendship.

"Did you take a look at yourself? What is going on?"

Gaëlla is already in his arms. Her Dad, her hero,

her ship's captain. She is ecstatic about the new sail-boat moored in the marina at Rochefort.

"It's beautiful!"

She is trotting along the deck, in the tender sun-light of approaching autumn. She was born on a boat, and spent her early years on board. I thought she might have forgotten, I'm afraid she'll fall, but on the contrary, she moves around the deck with a touching happiness.

It's true that it is a fine boat.

"Bernard, how did you manage to afford it?"

"My novel! I signed the contract and got a sizeable advance."

This is something new. I take a good look into his blue eyes; they are drowned in a fatigue I have never before seen in him.

"You're writing at last?"

He is writing. At least that's what he says, and what he must have convinced himself of. His earlier life, Africa, Senegal, his adventures as a skipper in the West Indies. Given all the time he's been thinking about it, vaguely speaking about it, advancing age must have decided him to do something about it. But with Bernard I'm always a bit wary. What he says is not always what he does. He looks too sad for some-one who's fulfilled himself as a writer. "Where's your contract?"

"In a safe deposit box, in Paris. You don't believe me? Why don't you believe me?"

"Yes, yes . . . I didn't know you could get so much

money with an advance, that's all. What exactly do you plan to do with the boat?"

"Get out of here, Louise. I'm sick of France, I've had it up to here. I'll head straight for Senegal, I'll do fine. I feel at home there, you know . . ."

"Bernard . . ."

He has understood. I don't like his sloppy, scruffy appearance, or his tired gaze, his drawn features, his almost brutal desire to leave, as if death were in pursuit of him.

"I've stopped drinking. Promise. Just a glass from time to time. And never at sea, that you know."

I know. Never at sea. But on land, that is what separated us, tore us apart. I don't have the insight of a trained psychologist, but the fifty-year old adventurer who's re-examining his life and suffers from depression—I could see that coming like a squall on the horizon.

Money problems, bankruptcy, the previous boat unpaid—all that quickly adds up to fraud. He could not stand being locked up on land, couldn't stand the humiliation. Violence was his way to deal with it, and I could not stand that new Bernard, in whom there was nothing left of the happy-go-lucky, carefree companion of our good years.

Two years we've been apart. How has he been living since I left? I cannot believe this story about author's royalties.

"I'm all right . . . I've seen my son and my daughter. But I just can't stand it here any more, I need space, freedom, do you understand, Louise? It's different, out there."

Senegal is where he spent his happy childhood, did his studies in architecture; it's the country of his roots. He wants a new start there.

"Come! Come with me!"

I don't feel like it. And yet I do. Life is no dream for me either. I have an aim: find work, an apartment, put Gaëlla in school, and then file a request to emigrate to Canada. We spent our vacation there this year, to have a look, and I liked it.

However, to emigrate, first you have to work legally in France for a year, and then file your request. In other words, comply with the system I've been fleeing for years. I chose freedom, I chose to wander from one country to another, doing small seasonal jobs, combining work with leisure, quite simply. Up until now I've always managed quite well. Gaëlla has everything she needs, and so do I.

I sold crepes and waffles in France, costume jewelry in the West Indies, worked as a hostess on cruise ships, made T-shirts and sarongs in Tahiti to sell them to tourists in Hawaii, California, and Mexico. I can do dozens of things with my hands and I've always made a good living, without getting caught up in the web of credit, taxes, retirement funds and all the rest. I've always needed to keep moving. Ever since I was a child I've dreamt of the ocean, of boats, of voyaging. For a long time I made do with a backpack and a passport. It's that simple.

But now Gaëlla is growing up and there's no one

waiting for me in France. No paycheck either, no apartment; no apartment, no work . . . The vicious circle. And on top of it the scornful looks of civil servants, as if they were saying:

"That will teach you to try and live any old way, and not behave like everyone else. What about taxes? And social benefits? And retirement? And your child's schooling? You think you can live as you please, trying to get away from the nine to five?"

So I said to myself, why not Rochefort, since Bernard is living here at the moment. Gaëlla will see her father, and it might be easier to find an apartment and some work here.

And in fact it was, but my daughter, used to the open spaces of North America, looks sadly at her surroundings, dragging her Barbie dolls from one wall to another.

"No, Mommy, I don't want to stay locked up in here. Why can't we go on Daddy's boat?"

Four walls, a confining space: this is something she is not used to. The cramped studio frightens her. Me too. And if Bernard is fed up, I must confess so am I.

"Come with me, Louise. I'll drop you off in Senegal and you can catch a plane back from there. Then you can decide what to do."

"School's about to begin, Bernard. I have to do something about it, for Gaëlla."

"Three weeks, Louise . . . what's three weeks in the life of a child?"

Not a thing; that's true. Even the school principal

in Rochefort, to whom I went for advice, does not make a big deal about it. I can buy notebooks and text-books and play teacher on board for a few weeks. I teach her so much already, and she's not behind. In the West Indies she went to kindergarten, so she's at the same level as other children her age.

And besides, this little girl adores her father. For a while now I have been surprised by her questions:

"Do you think you'll get married with Daddy again some day?"

"No, sweetheart. But that doesn't change anything for you, you'll see him often."

"Can you make me a little sister?"

"To make you a little sister Mommy has to find an-other daddy. Maybe later on."

"When is later on, Mommy?"

They are playing together, father and daughter; she is whirling in front of him, making her skirt spin, to be admired, and he applauds. She asks him ques-tion upon question about the boat; he's so proud of the boat.

Suddenly I've decided. Come what may . . .

If my mother were here . . . She has never been able to understand my restless temperament. For her, a girl must find a place to hang her pots and pans in a house somewhere, and then be good and wait while life goes by, with a sedentary husband, a bank account, and Sundays spent with family. And, above all, she must have financial security.

She is very wary of Bernard. In fact, she doesn't like him very much. If I had been listening to her since my divorce I would do better to settle down, to find my niche instead of leading this gypsy life. Bernard is a strange fellow, that's certain. But I have loved him, I have spent a large part of my life with him, we have good memories and bad.

At times I have the feeling I don't really know the man. I've known him when he was happy, free, at ease on the ocean, smiling, washing his socks, cooking, doing his own thing, and still full of attention for me. We shared the chores, and there was never any question that we wouldn't. We had met by chance, in Martinique. Actually it was his boat that I met first. When I think back on it, it was like a sign of fate.

I was trying to find someone who would be interested in buying my return ticket to France. That's a common practice in the West Indies. Whoever is headed back to Europe runs an ad, and whoever has decided to stay on sells him his ticket in order to have something to live on. A devil-may-care existence, says my mother . . . I fell in love with the empty boat. I had been looking at it from the dock; I was mysteriously drawn to it. I had the feeling that it had always been waiting for me there. When the owner showed up, it was Bernard. A friend of his had placed the ad. It's easy to speak to strangers out there, you end up telling your life story in no time. It all seems so natural. I said:

"I've just split up with my husband, we're friends now. He's going back to the States, and I'm staying on, but I feel a bit lost, I need some advice, like where the cheapest place to live is and what sort of work I can get?"

"I've got a job as skipper for a while," he replied, "stay on the boat if you like, it will give you time to think things through. If you look after the boat while I'm gone you'll be doing me a favor, and it's better than a hotel room."

The rest is a simple story. When he got back, I was on the deck holding my bag.

"There you go, the boat's all clean . . ."

I was proud. It was the first time someone had trusted me without knowing me. He gave me a big smile: "Stay, why don't you?"

It lasted thirteen years. I liked everything about him. He had already been around; he told me about his life as a Frenchman in Africa, he knew how to fly a plane, pilot a boat. He was a warm-hearted adventurer, he'd tried his hand at everything, he was full of life and love for others, always with a smile. He had studied art, he liked to read, to write, to listen to music. He had the education I didn't have. He was thirty-five, and I was twenty-one.

One day I discovered that he had a family, an ex-wife, and two children, and that he had not seen them in years. He complained that he had no news, that he had ruined the life of his children, that he knew virtually nothing about them. But when you leave without a forwarding address, what can you expect in return? It was up to him to look his past in the eye. It would seem he has done so now.

"So have you decided? Are you coming? We'll

leave on September 30. The boat is great, you'll see. I've taken her for her sea trials, she handles well, Louise."

His eyes light up at the idea of a trip for the three of us. I know how much he needs it. His troubles are over, and September 30 is a sort of symbolic date for him. At last he will have the right to leave French territory. He is no longer under judicial control. He has finally paid his debt to society, to France, for the fraudulent bankruptcy of which he was accused.

To cast off is like a release from prison. In other words, he can thumb his nose at the world. He also needs a crew member.

For a moment he is once again the same Bernard who said to me one day on the dock of the marina at Pointe du Bout:

"Stay . . . You don't need to commit to anything . . ."

At that time I was both disoriented and happy. For the first time I was going to fly my own wings, learn so many new things. My first marriage had been between two adolescents who had grown up together, and wanted to move out from home and live on their own.

My ex-husband boyfriend and I had made a good couple in the end. We had done what we wanted to do. He dreamed of music, I dreamed of boats. But apart from a Sunday sailing dinghy, I didn't know much about sailing.

Now it's different. I'm good at the helm, I know the sea, I've learned the ropes thanks to Bernard. It's been a while since I've been on board a boat, but it's not something you forget. The only difference is Gaëlla. She'll be six years old on October 29. When she was a baby, on our first sailboat, it was not a problem. She learned to walk on board. But we've been living on land since she was two and a half years old. I'll have to teach her to live aboard all over again.

My precious Gaëlla. My desired child, as I turned thirty. I can still hear myself saying to Bernard: "It's time, I'm reaching the age when a woman must have her child, Bernard."

I remember how passionately I spoke then. It was a turning point in my life. I felt great, I had energy, and the patience required to raise a child.

Such an urgent need to be a mother.

"You see, it's as if I were sitting in an armchair, taking stock, thinking to myself, well, you've done this and that, you've learned about life, you've made the most of it, now it's your turn to give life. Do you understand?"

He understood, but in the beginning he didn't want a child. He would talk about his own earlier life, the children he had not looked after. His remorse. Later, he said, we'll see, later . . . Until the day I left him, on an impulse. His hesitation, his half-refusal, were severing something vital inside me. It was, yes, something urgent, an obsession. A woman is not fully a woman until she has had a child. That is what she is made for. A belly is made to have children, breasts are for feeding. It was, quite simply, an animal instinct. I didn't want anyone to try and persuade me to the contrary. I could not wait any longer.

"All right then. If you don't want to, I can't force you. I'm leaving."

It was wintertime in Hawaii, December 1987. A very mild winter. We were both on board the *Petit Prince*, bought in Tahiti. And on other boats I could see people with children, happy children. Little future sailors, self-sufficient, open to the world. It did not look as if it were a problem.

His blue eyes were unhappy, a lost look, but he let me go; then one month later he said to me:

"Okay. If you want a baby, we'll have a baby. I want this baby too."

I knew the day of her conception. I felt it like a certainty, even before it was confirmed to me. And right after that I took on my role as a pregnant mother the way a nun takes her vows.

It was another world, another fabulous adventure. I gave myself to it, totally. I literally devoured Laurence Pernoud's baby book, *I'm Expecting a Baby*.

I read: you must walk half an hour a day, minimum; so I would get off the boat and walk up and down the docks.

I read: you have to eat such and such, so I ate it . . . You must swim; I swam. And yet, strangely, I really hate being in the water. However much I might like being above it, I feel out of place in it. But I nearly drowned when I was a child, and since then I swim with a certain apprehension.

I read: listen to music, relax, relax the baby too; I listened to music, stretched out on my berth, conscientiously, for "my daughter." Because it would be a girl, I was sure of that. I caressed my belly, immersing myself into this new life, overawed by the idea that this tiny microscopic thing I had been shown on the ultrasound was going to be a human being. I was already possessive, protective, full of love for her.

I wanted her to be born in the United States. An old fantasy of mine, the daughter of Sicilian immigrants; for her I had dreams of the entire world and of a dual nationality. Abroad, it is better to have to deal with an American consulate.

So Gaëlla was born in Oakland on October 29, 1988. Quite dark, like me; chestnut colored, like me. Bernard was surprised. He expected to see a little blond head that would look like him.

I breast-fed her for two and a half years on the boat. It was practical, and I had a lot of milk. And there she is, the baby, five years and a few months later. In her father's arms. Chatty as a magpie, hopping like a bird and not letting him out of her sight, her absent father; I can tell she has really been missing him.

She has only seen him very occasionally over the last two years. All summer, she has been pestering me:

"When are we going to go and see Daddy? When is he going to call?"

He would send her postcards that she would pin up in her room. He was always present, visible to her. She would ask those who knew her father, her friends:

"Do you like my daddy?"

She needed for someone other than me to tell her.

"I love you, Daddy. Do you love me?"

That is why I said yes. And for various other reasons, which came together, forming a circle, a circle of fate.

So that Gaëlla could make the most of her father. To really love him, touch him, invade him, immerse herself in his presence to last until our next meeting.

So that her father might be happy for a time with her, before setting out on new adventures, as they say in the comic strips.

So that this country of France that wanted no part of me—jobless, without a salary, a place to call home, with my living six-year-old in tow—would have to wait a little while longer. That I might have time to regain my strength before facing the want ads, government officials, landlords, employers. It's maddening how many papers you need in France. I hate all this paperwork.

And so that Bernard would not leave on his new boat with that sad look of the lone sailor abandoned by the entire world. He has frightened me with his depression, his sick complexion, his endless packs of cigarettes. And alcohol disguised as an anti-depressant.

The ocean has to be good for him.

There were a lot of things in favor of this decision and not much against. I even had a slight hope at the back of my mind. If I could find a way to settle in Senegal for a while? Not with Bernard, for sure. It was out of the question for us to share our lives any more. But Bernard the friend could still help me to find a solution other than that of being confined between the four walls of a maid's room. We would see.

Once the decision was taken, I was happy. Impatient to discover the boat, to get to know her gradually, to be at the wheel again, to feel the waves beneath me and breathe the air of this incredible freedom that life on the ocean gives. And watch Gaëlla learn once again to be a little sailor, with all that life on land gave her of the spoiled child. Her little mermaid, Ariel, and her multi-colored Barbies, her prince Ken, and her three snails found under a bush.

Three little snails. Gaëlla wants to take them onto her father's sailboat. Three snails at sea; it sounds like a poem by Prévert.

"Look, Mommy, there's the daddy snail, the mommy snail and the baby snail. You won't forget the lettuce, will you? And orange juice, and strawberry yogurts, and cakes, and . . ."

"Louise, you're pampering her, she's still in your apron strings! Come here, sweetheart, let me show you how it works. That's the wheel; when you want to turn to the left, you turn the wheel to port, and to starboard to go to the right."

You never set sail on a Friday; it's bad luck. We think about it at the time, superstitious like all sailors. Then we forget because we're happy. Gaëlla has put her three snails into a box, with the lettuce; she's chatting away with them the way she does with her dolls. My daughter is a chatterbox. Like me.

The boat must first leave the marina in Rochefort, wait for the tide to ebb, then go through the locks. The weather is neither good nor bad, a fair sort of weather for this time of year. One of Bernard's friends is buddy-boating with us as far as the Île d'Aix. We leave the marina with the appropriate slowness, motoring gently and quietly down. The smells from the land rise slowly for a while longer; we can see cows, houses, birds. It feels like a safe departure. There's nothing of the brutal tearing away that an immediate departure onto the open ocean can give. We slide gently into the evening, when we will go to sleep, moored to a buoy, tied alongside a friend's boat. The sea, the real ocean, is for tomorrow morning.

There are a few more things to check, and that's what our stop at the Île d'Aix is for. Bernard has made a lot of the preparations by himself. As I came on late, decided late, the only thing I could take care of was the food. He took care of everything else. The sails, the engine: I have nothing to fear in that respect. He has taken the sailboat out a few times to test it. The *Jan Van Gent* is in excellent condition: a new radio, a powerful engine, and, something new for us, a wheelhouse to shelter us from the wind and spray. This is the first time we have windshield wipers!

Bernard is proud of this boat, a 36-foot ketch with spotless sails, a roller-furling jib, heating, a shower. Very comfortable below, with a multitude of gadgets.

He is sitting at the wheel, happy as a clam.

"Look, she's steering herself!"

It's true, the boat behaves well. It always takes a certain amount of time to get used to a new sailboat. To find one's way, feel the boat, become a part of her. I don't know this one yet. The wheelhouse is the one thing which disturbs me somewhat. I'm used to being outside on deck, in my foul weather gear, the wind in my face, which may not always be much fun, but the feeling one has of departure is immediate. You become one with the ocean. The *Jan Van Gent*, with its glassed-in wheelhouse, gives me the impression that this is sailing for seniors, so well-protected.

"Aren't these windows dangerous? They don't seem to slide very easily and I think they're too big. Can you imagine being caught in a hurricane with these things? They could have provided some storm shutters! They're not even waterproof!"

"I'll look into it at the next stop, at Vigo. I'll have some plywood shutters made, or we'll replace them with Plexiglas. In the meanwhile we'll stay dry during our watches, that's something, isn't it?"

It's fine. Comfortable. A bit strange, all the same, this unaccustomed luxury. Once the windows are protected I'll feel better. I don't like these drops of water stealthily sneaking in, in the corners; and this glass vibrating. Bernard has every reason to be proud of everything else.

I think back on all our previous departures. We are used to sailing in warmer waters, under a bright blue sky. Here the sky is totally grey. I don't know this coast. I don't know Senegal either. Bernard knows the anchorage in Casamance. A quiet place, nothing dangerous. I trust him.

Beyond that, the future remains cloudy. Back to Paris, then what? We'll see. Gaëlla is so happy, she's having a great time. The tiniest thing makes her laugh. I have so much to teach her.

"Gaëlla, on a sailboat you need one hand for the

boat, and one for yourself. Don't play at Tarzan, swinging from the top of the door!"

She was swinging like a little monkey between the wheelhouse and the saloon.

"Gaëlla, don't leave your doll lying around in the companionway! On a boat you have to put everything away! Do you want Daddy to break his neck when he comes below?"

She learns quickly. No problems there. If I had been afraid she'd be sick, frightened or unsettled at the beginning, I was wasting my time. She takes everything in, plays, asks questions, sleeps like an angel, flutters between her father and mother, as if divorce no longer existed in her head. The boat is her nest, once again, the image of everything she holds dear. Daddy, Mommy and the sea.

She swims like a fish, though I can't; she eats while I'm never hungry when we first set off, and neither is Bernard. She wakes up when we change watch to go for some cuddles in her father's arms, then she comes to me.

Fish fascinate her, birds enchant her. She had her first birthday in California, her second one in Mexico, her third and fourth ones in France, the fifth in the West Indies. And the sixth? Why not—in Senegal?

To see her so happy, wolfing down her raviolis, without the slightest sign of seasickness, I do not miss the room with its hundred-fifty square feet, the toilet on the landing and the window overlooking a wall. All alone, if I kept my eyes closed, it might have been possible, but not with her. And even all alone—honestly! I cannot stand a fenced-in horizon, I need the sea, a river, something to look at, without barriers, beyond which there is something else, then something else again. I can't stand it when people say:

"Be careful, Louise. There's a barrier there . . . you can't go any further. Watch it, you're not allowed to do that, to go there . . ." I get the feeling I have been taken hostage. In the end, this last minute decision to leave has freed me from the anxiety which was beginning to stifle me. Like a gigantic "get lost" to all the barriers on earth.

The next morning, Saturday, there is no wind. Bernard makes use of the time to try out the engine. Nothing to report. I put the apples away, explaining to my daughter that if you wrap them in newspaper they won't rot. I unplug the fridge and we store the fishing lines in there. Usually we would store them aft, but this way they're close at hand. Besides, we don't keep anything in the fridge: everything rolls around in there, at sea. It's only useful in the marina. I go over my list of provisions.

"Gaëlla, you mustn't take anything to eat without telling us. Look, Mommy has made a list, and every time we use something we cross it off the list. Do you understand? If you eat all the cookies at once, you won't have any left for the rest of the trip."

My greatest fear is still that running up on deck she might trip. Already, when she was small and learning to walk, it was time for us to move back on land. You couldn't take your eyes off her for an instant. But now from the start her father has shown her how to walk, how to hold on. Don't run, don't lean overboard: she respects his orders and has gotten her sea legs with an ease which leaves us dumbfounded.

Everything is fine. We are surrounded by jellyfish, and Gaëlla draws colonies of them in a notebook with her felt-tip pens. There are a lot of fishing boats, pots everywhere, and we have to navigate carefully.

At the first customs boarding, Bernard complains: "Even at sea they won't leave you alone."

They take over an hour with their inspection, which is routine. The papers are in order, the boat is clean, and we set off again. Still no wind. We try out the VHF, we listen to the weather forecast, we look at the charts. An ordinary day.

Bernard's friend has left with his boat to head back to the Rochefort marina; "take care, bye bye," it always seems strange. Makes me feel like crying. He really is a friend. When we leave land, I always get the feeling I'm leaving someone behind. Then I immerse myself into the boat, with my daughter. It is important to go round it, go up, down, learn where things are kept, find one's place. A boat is like a human being, you have to speak to her, touch her, ask her silent questions, take note of her replies.

Bernard trailed a fishing line and caught a fish. It gave us a chance to teach Gaëlla that fish don't live in supermarkets. We are followed by dolphins for a while. It's life; it feels good. Every departure takes me back to the others—Tahiti, Hawaii, San Francisco, the day of the earthquake. We were there, fortunately in a protected marina.

Gaëlla doesn't stop for a minute. She changes clothes three or four times to show her father that she is pretty, that her skirt swings, that her shoes are this way or that way . . .

I love this day where we do as we feel, thinking, playing, tidying, dreaming. Each of us is happy. A sacred happiness, on a day like today.

First night at sea. Gaëlla eats well, better than on land, and goes to sleep. Bernard doesn't eat a thing. He's always like this, the first three days, he needs a certain time. I force myself to eat. You use up a lot of energy on a boat and I know I must keep some strength.

Still no wind, still on the engine, an incredible amount of traffic. This place is a real intersection, and the freighters pay about as much attention to the *Jan Van Gent* as to a straw; it's nearly always up to us to change course.

Sunday, we continue to plug along, no wind, on the engine. Gaëlla is fishing, doing her homework, talking with her father. Another customs check, by air this time. I show Gaëlla how to make signs on deck to tell them everything is fine. Before the European Union we used to go to the Port Captain for clearance: number of passengers on board, cargo, destination, papers, etc. This is no longer the case, but this freedom means that customs have to increase their vigilance on the ocean. Problems of drug traffic, dealers, illegal immigrants.

I'm doing well on watch. In the end it is not so unpleasant to be where it's dry, in a T-shirt, in this glassed-in wheelhouse. It makes me feel like I'm in an aquarium, but it's comfortable. The only problem, at night, is the shipping traffic. Sometimes I have to wake Bernard up to ask him what to do:

"Look . . . that one keeps changing course."

"What a jerk! Where does he think he is? We leave land to get some peace and quiet, and now look!"

I've never experienced this, on any ocean we've sailed. We constantly have to tack back and forth, not only because of the wind, which has risen, but because these vicious ships are headed straight for us, as if to say, "Get out of the way, I'm at work . . ."

We've planned to make Vigo our next landfall; it will take us four or five days. I cannot wait to get away from this floating freeway!

The sea is strange. There's not an awful lot of wind but you can't really tell where it's coming from. There's a swell; the water is gray. Bernard is having some problem with the radio. In order to check the weather, the easiest method is to contact a freighter and ask if they have any satellite information. This morning Bernard tried to get in touch with a freighter and they didn't respond. Then we passed another ship, Spanish, it might have been *La Pérouse*, but they didn't contact us either.

Wednesday October 5, in the morning, the wind is howling. It has begun to rain. Bernard decides to tack out to sea to avoid the coast. We should reach Vigo on the 6th, in the morning. We still have a ways to go, but the boat is handling perfectly. We've switched the engine off, the sails are fine, and the *Jan Van Gent* does not heel too much. Gaëlla is not even seasick.

I sleep when it is time to sleep; our watches are an hour long. Normally people have four-hour watches but I think that's madness. I can rest and recuperate much better in an hour than in four hours. That's the way Bernard and I have always done it.

In the evening we begin to pitch and bang around in earnest. Bernard has put a reef in. It was a struggle, with the mainsail. Impossible to head into the wind so we had to work with the wind abeam. A real exploit. I don't like this sudden change, however. We've seen this before, but without Gaëlla. When we set off we both slept in the forward cabin, for safety. This evening we change everything. Neither Bernard nor I are hungry, but Gaëlla is. The stove is on gimbals, and we have to secure the pot in order to heat up the raviolis she's so fond of. The apples roll back and forth constantly and this makes her laugh.

Ten o'clock at night. Bernard looks worried; there are hollows beneath his eyes. This squall has come upon us so quickly, in a few minutes everything has changed. He comes down to the saloon, pale, soaked.

"It doesn't look good, Louise. I'm trying to get someone on the radio to find someplace closer than Vigo, an inlet, but I can't get through to anyone. It's impossible to find out the direction of the bad weather."

"How far off are we?"

"Fifty miles, roughly . . . I just don't get it. There are plenty of calls on channel 16 as usual but no one is picking up."

This portable VHF radio does not carry as far as

the regular ones, but it worked fine with another sail-boat we passed just before the storm. Besides, we've been trying it regularly every day. We've spoken to trawlers, freighters, only quickly of course, since channel 16 is an emergency band and you can't talk too long, so you don't tie it up.

"There's nothing, Louise, no one's answering."

He wasn't expecting a cruise like you'd get in the West Indies, but he wanted to try out the sails, have a good time, and give us, too, a lovely trip; and instead, he's going to have to fight. Gaëlla. He's thinking of her, above all. We've been through stuff, the two of us. We've been through worse.

"Go get some rest, Bernard. You won't hold up, otherwise. I can handle the boat, I'll take your watch."

"No, it's up to me to be at the wheel, we'll head for La Coruña. That way we'll have the waves from the quarter."

I am worried, but still not too much. The boat is behaving well. Without the mainsail she has settled down, with a tiny bit of jib and the engine at mid-throttle.

"Bernard, you've got to get some rest. Be reasonable. I can take the wheel, you know that. Gaëlla's asleep, why don't you do the same."

He can't take it anymore. We have had to block the door of the wheelhouse, it was constantly banging. The hook doesn't hold. So each time he wants to go out on deck in a hurry he has had to climb through the port window. An irritating exercise. He rages against this stupid door lock.

"Things like this are dangerous . . ."

"Try to sleep, and if there's the slightest problem, I'll call you."

He finally agrees. I get up quietly, without waking Gaëlla, who has been asleep in my arms, and we go up to the wheelhouse. Bernard decides to lie down on the cabin sole, moving the folding seat to starboard.

I take the helm at 10:35 P.M. The boat rears up, the waves thunder by. With all this noise Bernard hardly sleeps. He opens his eyes and closes them again regularly; he's anxious. He listens to his boat, trying to figure out the struggle going on with the hull. He sees that it is hard for me to steer. Not that it is tiring, we have hydraulic steering, it's flexible, but because of the height of the seat I have to rest my feet on a heavy tool chest. In calm weather that's no problem, but in this tumult I lose my balance most of the time, my legs slipping out before me.

But still I manage, I can feel the waves unfurling, port broadside, I can sense them coming. The *Jan Van Gent* toils forward, slowly. I am exhausted by every wave we encounter, but I'm still in control. The boat is sturdy, the wave crashes down, sweeps the deck, the windshield wipers make their little back and forth motion, I hold on, my legs swing, then I start all over.

The moon has become enormous, the light on the mast is very bright and I say to myself, Louise, this is just one battle. In reality, it is war. I barely have the time to shout: "Bernard!"

It's not a wave, it's a wall. Ten stories of wave, a

tidal wave. And the thousandth of a second where I say to myself, "Oh no, have mercy, not that one . . ."

It has risen to port, and the boat is in the trough. I've seen it in nightmares, that wave, in my childhood, after hours spent reading stories of sailors and buried treasure, adventurers of the South Seas. Often I would wake up with a start, terrified by the watery giant about to sweep me away. I have been haunted by it.

"Bernard!"

The wall crashes down, the boat lies over, all the way to starboard, like a leaf. I am thrown from my seat with such violence that I picture myself already going through the wheelhouse. The sea is going to gulp me down, swallow me, bury me beneath tons of water. The sudden vision of this liquid wall in the halo of fire of the masthead light is so violent, at that moment, so powerful, that my brain spins, breaks away. My lungs are filled, ready to explode. Impossible to describe such terror, the way one's entire body is crushed. Not even time enough for simple fear. It is well beyond fear. I see myself drowned, I feel drowned, I have already died.

I want to breathe, I don't want to die like that. It's madness. I see myself doing a breast-stroke. I can hear something cracking; from what height have I fallen?

(Even today I cannot describe that wave. Words fail me. A wall. That is the only one I can find. To describe the height, the enormous size, the power. Nobody has been able to understand this wave, and every time I have tried to describe it there has been this frustration, and I can see that other people cannot see it as

I did. It was a liquid, dark wall, topped by another white wave at its crown. As high as the mast. A rolling, breaking wave; a killer.)

And then the enormous noise. Everything that was to port went flying at the same time, the cupboards opening, the supplies, cans striking the ceiling, water, water. The boat lies glued to the sea, and torrents of water pour into the wheelhouse, and the windows shatter. There is a boiling, a shrieking; something overwhelming, flying, exploding. I am afraid of being torn from the wheelhouse, and that is when I begin to panic.

The boat rights herself with a terrible slowness.

Chaos all around me. Food everywhere, jam, tomato sauce, peas, on every wall and bulkhead of the cabin.

And Bernard is getting up with difficulty; the heavy toolbox hit him right in the chest.

"Are you okay? Are you okay?"

"Okay . . ."

He does not seem to be hurt, but the blow must have been very painful. He looks at me: something like a nightmare in his eyes, a terrible distress. It hurts to see him like this. Am I the same? The same madness in my eyes?

Immediately I think of Gaëlla. She is still lying on the bunk in the saloon, brutally woken by the shock, but she saw nothing and does not know what is going on. She is soaking. The comforter took the shock, she's all right. I take her in my arms to reassure her, there is water up to the bunks, I can hear the noise of my boots in the cabin where toys are floating. Bernard joins me, holding his stomach, bent over.

"The engine's had it, the batteries too."

At that point I notice that he is, like me, covered with tiny scratches. The glass of the wheelhouse windows exploded, the way old windshields do, into a thousand microscopic fragments. One of my buttocks is hurting, I must have struck something when the wall of water came down on us.

Bernard doesn't know what hit him. If he had been at the wheel he would have understood, but stretched out on the floor as he was, dozing, he did not see what I saw.

The boat's a shambles now, a real nightmare. A strange chaos where everything is floating upside down. Gaëlla is crying.

The conversation between Bernard and me at this point is made up of short, hacked-off sentences, circling around our daughter. Rapid questions, rapid answers. The engine has stalled. The deck light is still working, the cabin lights too. The brand new inflatable, solidly lashed on deck, has exploded. It is half past midnight. The engine refuses to start.

We have to take stock: we are roughly forty miles offshore.

I don't know how much time we had before the second rogue wave. So strong it lay the boat on her side again and caused her to spin 180 degrees. Like a top.

Instinctively I put my head down, holding tight to Gaëlla. I don't know what I expected—another liquid wall. But we went down quickly, then rose again just as quickly.

This is definitely a sturdy boat.

Bernard is concerned about the liferaft. If a wave tears it off, we'll have nothing left. And there is always a third wave.

The seconds, the minutes trickle by to the clamor of the sea, with infernal slowness. I try to find a flashlight in the surrounding chaos, but we can't find a thing anymore. Bernard is looking too. We talk without shouting, in order not to frighten Gaëlla.

"Louise, we cannot risk a third wave. It would be impossible to get out at the last minute. If we were alone we could do it, but not with Gaëlla. I cannot take that risk."

"I don't want to leave the boat. You should never leave the boat."

I remember *Fastnet* 1979, that race off the coast of England where some of the sailboats were found deserted. Some sailors had died of cold in their foul weather gear; others had disappeared. Boats can hold out a long time, not men.

I don't want to leave.

"I sent out an SOS, Louise, they must have heard! We're near the coast. If we were on the open ocean, we wouldn't stand a chance, but here, they'll find us!"

My entire body, instinctively, rejects this solution. I feel myself splitting in two: one part of me is listening to Bernard saying, over and over, "There will be a third wave, it will be too late . . ." The other Louise sees, parading through her mind, empty sailboats, their skippers gone forever. It's madness! We mustn't! Yes, but that wave, that monster, if it comes back it will be to kill us. The third wave, the famous one, is always the worst, or so they say.

Some of the floorboards in the wheelhouse have lifted, you can see the drowned engine. I refuse to panic. Bernard is not really panicking, but he is tense, in shock, and the decision to be taken at this fateful moment belongs to him alone. He is responsible for both of us.

"I cannot even steer, we must have something caught in the propeller!"

"And if we put a line out to the liferaft? We could wait for the storm to grow calmer, and if the boat doesn't sink we could come back on board . . ."

"And if the wave throws us against the boat? If we lose the raft and the boat? What do we do then? Can you picture us in the ocean, the three of us?"

Still I resist. But the liferaft lashed to the roof of the wheelhouse is moving, the lines have loosened. If the next wave carries it off, we'll have no choice left at all. I am shivering, and so is Gaëlla. Bernard decides to climb on the wheelhouse to examine the lines.

"Put your harness on!"

Bernard puts his lifejacket on and fastens his harness. He has to wriggle to get out on deck through a port window, struggling with it for a moment before he is able to make it slide open.

God forbid that he falls in the water!

"Don't fall! I won't be able to get you out of there!"

It was silly but that's what I shouted. He didn't even hear me.

Noise above my head. He's taking care of the liferaft. I am holding the wheel, trying to bring her into the wind, but she hardly responds.

Long minutes go by, I can hear Bernard tramping around above us, then he finally comes back the way he went out, streaming with water, so pale.

"Get your things ready, let's go! I've tied the raft to the port stern!"

I look at him, stupefied, my eyes wide open. He has decided. Now it's too late. Once the liferaft is inflated, we have no more choice. We have to get into it.

"It's madness! You shouldn't have! Have you any idea how many people have been lost at sea because they did just that? Bernard, I did not agree . . ."

"Listen, Louise, we have to go. There were some lights, earlier, you saw them too! There are surely some fishermen nearby, we'll send off a flare from the liferaft, they'll see it!"

"Wait a bit longer . . . perhaps it will get calmer . . ."

"Wait for what? For the third wave to get us? It will be too late . . . the boat won't be able to take it, Louise . . . It can't take it . . . Think of Gaëlla! We can't get on board if all hell breaks loose. We've got to go now!"

It's all over. I've given in. I'm not pleased with myself, but in moments like this, it is the more convincing argument which wins. And above all, it is Gaëlla's eyes. Her fear. With a child on board you don't reason in the same way. All Bernard's arguments parade through my head at the same time. The coast is not far, there were lights from the fishermen, we sent our SOS, our flare. A bad moment to go through and then we'll be picked up. He's right. He must be right.

I dress Gaëlla in a track suit and some socks, her boots and lifejacket, explaining to her as calmly as possible what we are going to do. She is no longer crying, and she listens as I talk.

As for Bernard, he says he will take care of the food supplies. I see him fiddling in the open cupboards, lifting up soaked cardboard boxes.

"Where is the money?"

"Wherever you put it. In the Nescafé jar!"

"It's not there! Did you take it?"

"Of course I didn't! You'll find it!"

As for me, I hastily gather up a few papers and our passports, and I stuff a duffle bag with towels, warm clothes, gloves, bonnets, scarves. My daughter is calm, because we are calm.

"Mommy, are you taking some orange juice?"

I grab a bottle of orange juice. At the same time I fill an empty bottle with fresh water.

"Mommy! Are you taking cookies?"

I stuff a package on top of the clothing. I don't take care of the rest. Bernard said:

"I'll take the food and the cigarettes!"

The sacrosanct cigarettes. He's getting irritated, he hasn't found the money, and in this shambles there's nothing surprising about that. I get angry in turn.

"Forget it! You must have put it somewhere else!"

"I'm not going to forget twenty-five-thousand francs! Louise, we'll need it! Are you sure you didn't put it somewhere else? You didn't take it?"

"I told you I didn't!"

There's something surrealistic about this argument, amidst the pounding waves and the urgency of getting ready to abandon ship. He's wasting valuable time, valuable calmness. I know the money is important, but if it went overboard, through the wheelhouse . . .

He gives up, despairing.

I see him pick up a plastic bucket; he's filling it, rapidly, while the boat pitches and rolls, and we find it so difficult to hold on in the chaos of the saloon, in this water swishing a mass of objects from one side to the other. I'm too busy with Gaëlla to look at what he is doing.

"We'll go out this way . . . you see . . . Mommy will go out first, then Daddy will help you . . . don't be scared . . ."

But I make one last attempt with Bernard to try and delay the moment when we will have to climb into the liferaft and be lost to the storm.

"We could connect the raft to the boat with lines tied one to the other, we'd have a good length, four or five hundred feet, don't you think?"

He has his back to me, wedging a bottle of rum in the plastic bucket. He grumbles:

"If it got really bad, we wouldn't have time to cut

the mooring lines, they are too thick . . . Hurry up, Louise . . ."

The image of the *Jan Van Gent* sinking inexorably into the sea, dragging us along with it like a parcel . . . I shiver.

In my mind I also rage against the wheelhouse, as high as a watchtower. If it weren't for the wheelhouse the waves would have passed over the boat without causing any damage, like a simple sailboat for example. Damned wheelhouse—all these shards of glass, everywhere, the feeling of drowning that seized me earlier when the boat lay over on her side, it was so horrible. I am soaked. Neither my boots nor my life-jacket can prevent my teeth from chattering. I've given up the idea of putting my foul weather gear on top of everything, I wouldn't be able to move.

"Hurry up, Louise."

"The fishing lines! We must take them!"

"There will be some in the raft! Hurry up!"

The raft is tied to the hull. We have to go out through the sliding window to port, move along the deck to reach the raft. I have never seen a liferaft in-flated. I'm suddenly terrified of the thing. Six feet across. We're going to close ourselves inside that thing, and then what? Have we made the right choice?

He has persuaded me, I obey, but in some corner of my mind I am still thinking, "This is a bad thing . . ."

And in another corner: "Gaëlla. He's right, for Gaëlla. We cannot risk Gaëlla's life . . ."

The raft is not tied on in the right direction; the

usual opening, through which one is supposed to enter, is facing out to the sea. In front of me is the hole for catching fresh water. A sort of cone-shaped tunnel in the canvas. It is not meant to let a body through easily.

Bernard says to me, very quickly:

"Go ahead, I'll pass Gaëlla over to you first and then the bags!"

My daughter's black eyes are wide with terror and she begins to scream: "Help! Help!"

"Gaëlla, sweetie, don't shout, no one can hear you!"

"I don't want to go! I don't want to go in there! I want to go in the dinghy!"

The dinghy is the inflatable which was lashed on the coach house and which exploded with the wave. She's used to the dinghy, she went out for rides with her father before we set off.

I climb over the lifelines, holding with one hand, and twist myself around to dive through the tunnel. I force my way through with difficulty, legs first, my head outside, while the damned raft never stops moving in every direction.

Once I'm in there, closed inside this tiny, round dome, I hear Bernard's voice, stifled by the clamor of the waves:

"Take Gaëlla, Louise! Hurry up!"

I pull my daughter over, forcefully, by her legs; I make her slide through as I did, and she continues to cry.

"I don't want to . . ."

Her lifejacket gets stuck, and it takes all my strength to pull her towards me.

"Easy . . . easy, sweetheart. You'll be okay . . ."

I can barely see her little round face, her wide, frightened black eyes; I can sense her trembling mouth, her chin wrinkled in sorrow.

Am I thinking of anything in particular at this moment? No. I don't think so. I act, I settle my daughter into the corner of the raft, under the little orange light. Rapid, precise gestures. I realize that Bernard will not be able to squeeze through that stupid hole. And the opening is on the other side. I call out to him:

"Pass me the bags and turn the raft around! You tied it on in the wrong direction!"

In fact, the opening of the raft had been put in the wrong place to begin with.

He struggles for a moment before he manages to swing it around. In the meanwhile great masses of seawater cause him to waver; he hangs on, growing exhausted. Finally he is able to slide through the opening; I see him take his knife from his boot.

"What are you doing!"

"I'm cutting the line before we crash against the hull."

The blade slices through the rope, and he throws the knife overboard.

"Why did you do that? Why did you throw it overboard?"

"The blade could puncture the raft!"

No time to reply; in a few seconds we are thrown far from the sailboat. I can make out the masthead light, flashing to the rhythm of the waves; then it grows distant and disappears, taking life with it. I could cry. The *Jan Van Gent* gave birth to this round bubble, so light that we feel every furious splash of water beneath our buttocks. The boat cut the cord, the umbilical cord; the boat is abandoning us.

Five seconds. It's so quick; we have left her behind so quickly.

I feel that we are so small, three tiny larvae thrown onto the ocean. I say nothing. It smells like rubber and sea water; the little lamp throws a faint light onto our tiny dwelling space. At times, through the opening, I can see lights in the distance, so far away, so faint.

Bernard sets off a flare. We wait for a moment, our necks stretched in the direction of those hopeful lights.

Nothing. Now the lights have disappeared, the rubber bubble is turning on itself, in the stormy night.

Where is the boat? Will she reappear suddenly above us? Crush us? We look at each other in silence.

A wave wakes us brutally from this short, strange apathy. It penetrates, swishing, through the opening, soaking all our things in one second.

We have to close the opening to the raft, tie the flap to its three fasteners. One in the middle and two on the sides. I struggle with the thing until I realize that the flap which is supposed to be the door has a strap which must first of all be passed through the buttons on the outside of the raft. Nothing is practical in this raft. There are no nets to stow the bags and nothing to hold onto.

We are tossed around incessantly. Bernard settles Gaëlla down in the middle, and we sit on either side of her to stabilize the raft. I look through my bag. The cookies are a sodden mush and I throw them overboard so it won't make a mess on the bottom. Even in a state of panic I cannot stop myself from tidying house. Then I locate a leak in the cone-shaped rainwater intake.

I busy myself with fixing it as best I can and tying it up. The wave soaked us, and there is a small lake splashing in the bottom of the raft.

I caress Gaëlla's face; she is no longer crying and looks at both of us with her serious air. I smile to her; smiling is my weapon, my defense, my way of struggling against adversity. I give her a kiss. I always need to touch her, to cuddle her, to caress this little bit of woman I brought into the world.

"You are not grumpy, sweetheart, are you?"

Bernard looks very pale to me, but the light in here does not make us look our best. We look like corpses. We can't stand up. We have to watch every move we make. And it's horrible not to be able to see the sky, to be shut inside this thing, hunched over like toads.

"Are you all right?"

"I've got a bruise in the stomach, but I'm all right . . . don't worry . . . And you?"

"My bum . . . I don't know where I hit myself, but otherwise I'm okay . . ."

All night we try to sleep, but the waves leave us no time. The bubble threatens to capsize at any moment, to turn us upside down. We have to keep everything balanced on the wobbly floor, curve ourselves against the rubber rings, spread our arms out, let the wave pass under us and get ready for the next one. Most of the time the wave pushes against us, throwing us onto each other or making us spin like a top. Another mistake: we did not take time to set up the sea anchor to stabilize us. The cold is beginning to numb us quite severely, and water is getting in. There must be a leak somewhere. The bottom of the raft is splashing, we are sitting in sea water all the time. We must try to sleep. I manage to drift off for ten minutes and wake up when necessary. Which is often the case, every time Bernard says,

"Watch out, here comes another one!"

Our cadaverous faces, this unreal light, this enclosed space, the incessant dance of the waves, our efforts to keep the raft stable . . . At one point I thought, ridiculously, "It's like Disneyland."

Did we do the right thing? Shouldn't I have persuaded Bernard to stay on the boat, instead of letting him convince me to leave? I think about it all night long, while the sea plays with us in this rubber bubble as if we were a floating insect. While I watch my daughter curl her body up in the middle of the raft, and we lie like puppets pulling against our invisible strings.

I think too about the SOS. Someone must have heard us; in the morning, a freighter will find us.

The *Jan Van Gent* has surely sunk by now. Why did this happen to us? Why this brutal storm? I certainly did not expect a sea of glass, everyone knows this region is one of westerly winds, sudden squalls.

I think, then I sleep a few minutes, I cling onto the rings, and it starts all over.

Dawn. Thursday October 6, a pitiful sun was trying in vain to get past the layer of low gray clouds just above us. I lifted the flap to look outside, with the hopes of seeing in the distance the massive form of a freighter. We went past so many, even just yesterday.

Nothing. A leaden desert. We are drifting westward, a bad sign. The sea is still rough. Bernard is exhausted, his hands are pale with cold, the skin shrivelled like mine, but he tries to sound cheerful.

"Let's get warm."

We are tossed around a bit less. He gets out the bottle of rum. Gulps some down and passes me the bottle, and I too swallow the equivalent of a capful. It heats me up, momentarily, my throat at any rate.

"Are you asleep, Gaëlla? Are you asleep, honey? Do you want some orange juice?"

I rub her little hands to get the circulation going.

"Do you want some water?"

She mumbles that she's sleepy. I insist for a bit with no result. I don't know if she really wants to sleep or if she's sulking. She is in shock, in any case.

I am beginning to feel all the painful effects of last night's thrashing. I check by moving my leg in every direction; nothing is broken. But I must have a tremendous bruise on my bum.

Bernard watches me, also making faces. He is holding his stomach, gently rubbing his chest from time to time.

"It was the toolbox, I got a direct hit. It's nothing, it'll get better."

It is then, in the early morning hours, that we go through what we've got. First of all I check the clothes in the duffle bag, and our papers. The towels are soaked, I wring them out; the sweaters too. It takes me a while before I turn to the rest.

I reach for the plastic bucket that Bernard said he would fill. A carton of cigarettes, completely soaked, some matches in the same state, the bottle of rum, and nothing else.

"Bernard!"

I remember him telling me, "I'll take care of the food and the cigarettes." It was while I was getting Gaëlla dressed. I see him, rummaging in lockers, everything thrown about by the wave, the lockers where our supplies were.

"Bernard! There is nothing here!"

He looks at me, dumbfounded. He makes a face. As if he were shrugging his shoulders, helpless.

I am completely flabbergasted. I want to scream something, but nothing comes from my mouth. Scream, but what? This is not the moment to start an argument. We'll have all the time we need back on land to tell each other off. But still, I'm really pissed off.

"You thought about your cigarettes! Your god-awful cigarettes!"

They are so thoroughly soaked that I would be surprised if he could smoke one.

So we hunt through the orange bags which contain the survival kit.

A pair of scissors, a dull-bladed knife, some gauze strips, lots of gauze strips. Two sponges, a plastic bailer, a tube of antiseptic cream, some packets of fresh water—the equivalent of two liters—a sea anchor, two flares and some smoke devices.

"The flares are wet."

"The smoke devices too."

The last things are the rope and hoop which let you right the raft when it capsizes.

This bubble is supposed to be unsinkable, provided the raft is properly inflated, but it does capsize.

The rest is discouraging. Sea-sickness tablets, all in a pulp. A light which is supposed to be an SOS signal, but it doesn't work. Two wooden paddles, a repair kit with a tube of glue, "to be used only when the raft is dry."

I have no idea how the raft itself is to be used, the instruction manual is written in Flemish, in tiny letters, as is the Flemish dictionary that comes with it.

The only important thing is the pump, in good shape, fortunately, to keep the pressure in the rubber rings. No survival rations.

"Is that it, Bernard? Nothing to eat?"

"No."

"A mirror?"

"No."

"Fishing line?"

"There isn't any . . ."

I am overcome by rage at that point.

"I wanted to take them! You told me to forget it! You told me . . ."

"Normally there should be some."

"Normally? You know what you should have done, normally? Normally you were supposed to take care of the food! Normally you should have checked the liferaft! You could still have done it when it was tied to the boat!"

This "normally" is Bernard all over. With his sad eyes, like a dog who's been beaten. Punished, unhappy. He has a way at times of getting himself into the craziest situations and making me feel sorry for him to boot.

"They were right there, within reach, the fishing lines, in the fridge. We put them there on purpose."

"We won't even need them, Louise. They'll find us."

I am one of those people whose anger explodes and then subsides immediately. It's like sleep, a quick shot, and then I wake up. But even if I am calm on the outside, that does not stop my brain from racing at a hundred miles an hour. I try to get a grip on the information coming at me from all sides. Bernard is, morally, in very bad shape, and physically he's having a hard time coping. I think I know why. He has hardly eaten a thing since we left. Smoked, yes, swallowed a bit of coffee too, but that is not what you need in your stomach to be able to make it through. Fortunately

Gaëlla ate well last night, and I managed to get enough down to not feel hungry right away. So . . .

My only comfort is that we have the orange juice, and the extra bottle of water which I brought. And there's the rum. On the paper which says "survival," attesting to our disaster, I can just make out the words of advice: "Do not drink sea water. Do not drink urine." Okay. The inventory's over. We have to get organized. We'll tidy up, we'll take our boots off so we can free our feet from this damp, icy prison. We check the amount of water, to ration it. And finally we stream the sea anchor, which gives us more stability. It feels good.

"Two or three days. I say that two or three days is the maximum we'll wait to be picked up."

The sky is so overcast that no plane could see us. There are counter-currents, the waves are very close together and still bounce us around. The sea is so gray, so empty. I refuse to be overwhelmed by this grayness. I complain, just to keep going.

"This light is driving me mad, you can't even switch it off during the day! I wonder how it works."

"With batteries, I think, it lights automatically when the raft inflates."

"Are you in pain?"

He stretches out as best he can, his arms hugging his chest, his foulies over him.

"A bit. It'll pass."

I watch him struggle over a cigarette that he is trying to dry out, hopelessly. The entire carton wasted, no hope. But he continues to insist, "The coast isn't far, I bet that tomorrow night we'll be sleeping in a bed."

I will never forget that wave that knocked us flat as a pancake. I'll never forget the moment when the *Jan Van Gent* disappeared, with her mast light, taking away all the food, the fresh water, life itself.

I am angry with Bernard. I bury this feeling deep inside for the moment. I try not to tell him. Under normal conditions I would talk about it, I would argue for as long as it takes. But all alone, the three of us in this orange bubble which will decide our fate, I keep quiet.

For the first time in my life the words, "It's too late," take on such significance. The sea is merciless in its revelations. It knows how to punish human error.

CHAPTER THREE

The Silence of the Sea

T HE SEA IS SILENCE. A silence of smells and sounds. If a ship is upwind, you can smell the freighter's smoke from a long way off; you can hear, even before you see the ship, the humming of its engines.

I can smell nothing other than the nauseating odor of new rubber, can hear nothing but the relentless pounding of the waves beneath my body. These crumbs of tobacco floating in the water like a brownish gruel disgust me. Gaëlla is asleep. Scowling.

We are arguing, the two of us, in muted voices.

"That's all you could think about! Not a single can of food, nothing . . . when I think of everything there was on board! I *asked* you, Bernard . . . You said, 'I'll take care of it!'"

He lowers his head like a kid caught in the act.

"What can I do now? We're in shit up to here, I know, it's my fault, I know . . . What can I do?"

He will not look me in the eye. Usually he looks people in the eye.

"A carton of cigarettes—what selfishness!"

It is hard for me to keep quiet. But it is vital, for Gaëlla's sake. It's pointless adding to her anxiety with a fight between her father and mother. In mid-ocean, a family quarrel resonates into the void, hollow, stupid. But because I am trying to clean the filth which is mixing with the sea water, sticking to clothes, becoming embedded between the rings, I feel a nausea of words come over me all of a sudden.

Something more serious is there to alarm us. The raft is filling with water and we have to bail once again, using the sponges. After half an hour of this tedious work, the bottom of the raft is empty of water. Bernard relaxes for a moment, so do I, we cannot take our eyes from the rubber.

It starts again.

"There's a leak somewhere."

Gaëlla is still sleeping, curled up like a little cat, her head in her knees. And water is oozing all around her. It brings tears to my eyes. We go over all the rings circling the raft. With our fingers, slowly, moving carefully, bent over since we cannot stand up, watching out for any unexpected gesture on the part of the other which could upset the center of gravity and cause us to capsize.

"Shit! I was sitting on it!"

Bernard has just put his finger on a microscopic orifice beading stealthily with seawater.

It is terrifying, such a tiny, translucent threat.

"Can we fix it?"

"With what? This goddam glue won't harden if the raft is wet, you saw the instructions! Bloody clever their stuff when you're lost at sea!"

The only solution is to remain stretched out next to the hole and to raise the bottom cloth to keep it from coming in contact with the sea. A hopeless solution: we are constantly sitting in water. Added to our forced immobility, the damp cold air is making us totally numb.

I'm going to make a mattress with the towels, the lifejackets and the clothes, which we'll have to wring out carefully, twist and then arrange into a vaguely protective layer. In this way I find myself somewhat insulated. Gaëlla takes refuge against me, sleepy and grumpy. I have no idea what time it is. Time is of such importance that it ends up having no importance at all. Waiting is a hypnotic state.

I am stupefied and furious at the same time. Furious at watching him try, for the nth time, to dry a shapeless cigarette, strike a sodden match, while we don't even have a jar of jam or a single can of food, nothing solid to ingest. He could have taken *anything*, at random. Especially for Gaëlla. For myself I don't care so much. I am never really ravaged by hunger, I can keep going on a tomato, or a crust of bread. A swallow of fresh water or a quarter-capful of rum fails to remove the sticky feeling from my mouth.

"As soon as we're back on land, we'll have a great party. I'll take you to a restaurant, and we'll stuff ourselves with all kinds of things."

He takes banknotes from his wallet and spreads them out on the rubber ring. He must have rescued about three thousand francs. Convinced that we'll be out of this by nightfall, tomorrow at the latest, he talks to himself about our rescue. At the time, I believe him, of course. His SOS, the nearby coast, the number of freighters we passed on the preceding days: it all seems, logically, to warrant optimism. But there is one image which does not leave me, that of the *Jan Van Gent* fleeing into the night, in the howling of the wind and waves. Reality. Where has she drifted to? Or how has she sunk, if she has sunk?

As I think about all this I go over our injuries. Gaëlla is okay, that's the main thing. As for me, the wheelhouse windows have caused some damage, cuts on my arms and legs which are now stinging from the seawater, but nothing really to be too concerned about. But I do find myself shifting constantly from one buttock to the other, and I have a pain in my right side.

"Show me."

I twist myself round with difficulty so that Bernard can have a look at the painful spot; he concludes that I have a superficial cut along with a big bruise. So I'm all right, basically. Bernard is worse off. Not only is he covered with scratches but the slightest movement causes him to wince in pain. His stomach? His abdomen? His ribs?

"Where exactly does it hurt?"

"My chest. Or my stomach. It hurts to touch it, but don't worry about it."

But on the contrary, I do worry. He's acting the strong, brave man, but he looks awful. He's so pale, as if all the blood had drained from his face, beneath his beard. I don't like it. He has grown old all of a sudden. His eyes, the hollowness of his cheeks, his two clenched fists, show how wounded he is.

I recall little else of that first day on the raft except for the tobacco leaves: my rage against that tobacco, and the pitiful inventory of our survival gear. How we have *nothing*—that's the stupidest thing.

And also the great silence between Bernard and myself. Gaëlla dozes most of the time, sulking.

"What about my dolls?"

"We'll find them again, or we'll buy some new ones, don't worry."

She goes back to sleep, then wakes up with a start.

"Mommy, I need to go wee-wee!"

Not so easy to go wee-wee in this living sausage. For Bernard it is relatively easier, all he has to do is open the flap and relieve himself overboard.

A cut-off plastic bottle will do as a chamber pot for Gaëlla. The blade of the survival knife is not very sharp, but Bernard has managed to make the small container; now I hold Gaëlla balanced over the "potty." Her urine smells strong; she hasn't drunk enough since last night. I don't worry too much about it, I've just noticed it, that's all.

Operation "wee-wee" proves much more complicated in my case. I have to remove my foul weather jacket, slip down the suspenders of my overalls, slide my underpants down and hang onto a strap attached to the raft. The cold grips me immediately.

When I need to go again a little later on I give up altogether on this acrobatic exercise, both exhausting and dangerous for our balance.

"Mommy, you've gone wee-wee in your underpants! It's all hot!"

It's disgusting, but so what. I don't give a damn. I prefer this minor humiliation to being cold and to the risk of upsetting the raft. Dignity and modesty don't mean a thing on this gray and hostile liquid desert, tossing us about as it pleases. The sun is about to go down and the day has passed, strangely, without anything of greater significance happening. Until Gaëlla begins to complain:

"I'm hungry, Mommy. Tell me, Mommy, why aren't there any ships?"

Her father has been telling her all along that a ship would find us.

"Where are the ships, Mommy?"

The moment I open my mouth to voice my reproach, something paralyzes my lips. There's nothing Bernard can do. So I hang onto the hoop and raise the flap to look at the sky and reproach God. Tell him off for Bernard, for myself. Because I do reproach myself. But it's all mixed up in my mind, and I don't remember thinking about anything at that particular moment, just shouting:

"What have we done to you? Why us? Why are you punishing us like this? What wrong have we done? You have no right to make a child suffer! No right!"

A little hand clings to me. Gaëlla has crawled up behind me and is shoving her fist outside; like her mother, she's giving God a piece of her mind.

"I want a sausage! A cold one! I want some chewing gum, and I want . . . a sausage! Bad Jesus! Bad!"

Bernard thinks we're hysterical.

"Calm down, for Christ's sake!"

I sit back down and Gaëlla lies on top of me.

"What good does it do to insult God? You want him to really get mad at us? You'd do better to say a prayer."

I pray. Something like: "Please, dear God, our fate is in your hands, make a ship find us, make it change course, or send us an airplane or a helicopter."

It's naive. It's superstition or belief, I'm not sure which, but I need to speak to whatever is above our heads. An entity deciding for or against us. There must be something. Call it what you like, Fate, Jesus, God, bad luck or merciful salvation. Help us, damn it!

My tantrum against the heavens has worn me out. But I can't give up, in my head. Obstinacy is in my nature. I am convinced that if you really want something and don't let go of your concentration, you'll end up getting it.

"I'll make it, Bernard. We'll get through this."

"You'll make it. You're right. Help is on the way, I know you'll make it."

That evening, that night, I'm not sure when, he says to me, triumphantly: "Look!"

He has managed to light two cigarettes and passes one to me. It's so cold and damp that the warmth of the first puff is a benediction from the very heaven I was cursing. A small sign linking me to earth, to the world of the living, to elsewhere. If I close my eyes I can imagine land, human beings, a dry place. I swallow the smoke, I eat it with my bronchial tubes. This damned cigarette is actually giving me hope.

Then it's time to fall back into the brine. Bail. We have to bail every hour, just about, mechanically. Then Bernard uses the pump to blow up the rings. It's so exhausting and he is getting increasingly short of breath. I can tell he's suffering. In the bleary fading light his face frightens me. A ghost. Pity and anger mingle incessantly in my head. At times I want to shout:

"So much the better, all this is your fault!"

It wouldn't take much for me to tell him everything I've had on my mind since we split up. The failures: his life, our life as a couple, his unending money problems, his thoughtlessness, his depressing weakness. His lack of seriousness in this whole business. If . . . he had taken food, if . . . he had grabbed the fishing lines. With those 'ifs', I condemn him out of hand. But there is also tenderness, and pity. He is suffering. He needs a bed, blankets, a pillow, loving care.

"I'm glad you're here with me, Louise."

I fall asleep dreaming of a bed. My arms go round my daughter's body; her weight is making me numb. I dream of a palace, just to get through, so that my thoughts don't short-circuit.

Friday. It's Friday, October 7. Water is lapping underneath me and this wakes me up, and Bernard, too.

Daylight is filtering, weakly, through the orange rubber. I put my head out and see nothing but a hopeless gray. We have to bail again. My sleeves are sodden, I roll them up to pick up the two distress flares which we had been trying to dry on the rings; they've rolled into the water. I put them back. And I bail. Gaëlla is still sleeping; I move slowly so I don't wake her up. As long as she's asleep she doesn't know what's happening. That is, nothing. No one is coming to rescue us.

"Tonight . . . You'll see, tonight we'll be in a bed! No, a restaurant first! We'll stuff ourselves . . . I'm sure of it, they're looking for us . . . yesterday, well, it was a bit too soon, but from here on . . ."

Let God hear you, Bernard . . . I hope to Heaven that you are right.

"Let's dry the laundry . . . You pass me the clothes and I'll spread them out on the roof . . ."

Towels, sweaters, gauze strips.

"There's a bit of wind, that should help them to dry."

An empty horizon. Bernard lies down again, exhausted by the effort. He closes his eyes.

"I wonder where the boat is now. You know, Louise, if we find her someday I'll fix her up . . . However much time it takes, I'll do it! We'll set off for Senegal again."

Has he gone mad? He made us get off the boat, and now he's talking about finding her, fixing her up? What the hell is he playing at?

"Don't count on me! I don't give a fuck about your

boat. I'll never set foot on board a boat again! And neither will Gaëlla!"

Bad. I am bad, but the absurdity of the situation is too much for me. We've got nothing to eat, almost nothing to drink, and when Gaëlla wakes up and asks for something, what am I going to say to her? That Daddy is going to patch up the boat one of these days and we'll go off to eat bananas in Senegal? I don't understand men. And of course now he's in a mood. Calm down, Louise. I have to find something to do. Some cleaning up, pick up the flakes of tobacco one after the other. This forced immobility is going to drive me mad.

Bernard is going through the papers I snatched willy-nilly, looking at our passport photos: disjointed memories to occupy one's eyes and hands. When Gaëlla wakes up she asks to have a look at the pictures, too. Then once the game is over she asks to do something else. My address book is wet, but the pen is working.

"Let's write the alphabet, sweetheart."

She sets to work, complaining about the wet paper, which tears, and so I give her pieces of gauze strip which have dried, more or less, in the wind. At least the pen doesn't go right through them.

Then we set about gathering up the laundry, then we bail. That's the hardest, the most tiresome, the water constantly leaking in. To go faster we use our boots. Time goes by in this way, it's slow work, bailing, slow work watching your every movement, slow work moving around bent in two, stiff and numb, gesture upon gesture.

"We didn't bring a comb, Mommy!"

No toilet bag, that makes me think of toothpaste. We could have chewed on the paste, at least . . .

"I'm hungry, Mommy . . ."

"I'm hungry too, we must be patient, sweetheart."

Bernard thinks he's witty: "You did want to go on a diet."

He sees my angry look and adds: "Still, you're pretty like that, with hollow cheeks."

I wonder what I look like at this moment. Hollow cheeks, already? I must be frighteningly ugly. Pure habit, I run my fingers through my hair to untangle it, pass my tongue over my lips, then over my teeth; I've got a dull taste in my mouth and my stomach is tied up in knots from cramps.

Gaëlla looks at me, pleading. What can I do to calm her hunger? Chew on paper . . . on gauze strips . . .

"Wait, I know what we'll do, you can sit on my knees, and you can suck, like when you were a baby."

To give her my breast; that's all I can do. I fed her for a very long time, until she was two and a half, back then, we were sailing along the Mexican coast and you couldn't always drink the water so my milk was the easiest solution. Gaëlla remembers the movement of her head, to one side, she looks content, the happy look of the baby she once was and still is. She sucks. Then she lets go, disappointed:

"There's no milk."

"I know, but just pretend there is. Pretend that you're drinking Mommy's milk, think hard, very hard, and you'll see, it will calm your tummy down."

For me this is both moving and disconcerting. Moving because forgotten sensations are suddenly there again—the happiness of holding my baby, of caressing her hair, of speaking softly to reassure her. And disconcerting because I know how useless, how empty my breasts are. But if God made an effort? If he gave Gaëlla the milk she hopes for? A miracle, you never know . . .

The miracle is that she has fallen asleep holding onto my breast. I can pull down my T-shirt, my jacket, and look at her peaceful face. I have nothing else to offer her, only peacefulness.

The wind has risen again and the waves are tossing us from crest to trough; the ocean is whistling and shrieking beneath us, the noise is tiring, like that of a saw. Bernard says, all of a sudden:

"I hear a radio! Louise, listen!"

I can hear it too. A sort of crackling somewhere. Where? In the raft? On the water? Above or below? We look for it, listen closely, ready to hear voices, music, something living; our hope is so great.

"It's not possible, it's not a radio."

"Yes it is, listen."

"A leak? Maybe the tubes are deflating?"

"No, listen, Louise, listen. It sounds like the shrieking radio of a freighter. The sound is traveling over the water."

We couldn't find it. I still don't know what it was.

Joy enfolded us for a few minutes, the time it took to examine the horizon. Then we were afraid that we were delirious. Hearing imaginary sounds, the way one sees mirages in the desert.

"We have to talk, Louise, we have to keep our minds working."

"How do we do that?"

"What color is your jacket? Don't look, just answer."

"Green."

"Your turn, go ahead, ask questions."

"The color of your boots?"

"Blue. My turn. What day is it?"

The game goes on. He tells me everything he did to decorate the *Jan Van Gent,* the little pictures he didn't have time to hang in the saloon. At times doubt still comes over me: did he really write a novel? Did he really buy that boat on his own? He didn't insure it; it was impossible because of some document that was missing. How is he going to get out of this, financially? Supposing he does, some day, find the salvaged hull—what state will it be in?

I think about this, full of doubts, then forget, because it's not the time for this type of worrying. Gaëlla chews on the plastic of a half-packet of water as if it were chewing gum, to trick her hunger. She tears a piece off and hands it to me: "Here, Mommy, let's share it."

Why not. I chew away too, for the sake of the illusion, to get my saliva going. I'm hungry, my stomach aches, but that's not the worst thing. We all have stomach aches. I explain to Gaëlla that it's not that serious.

"You're hungry, so your tummy is protesting, it's getting mad and it's clenching. But you'll get over it. It won't take long. Tell your tummy that it will just have to wait."

"But I'm hungry!"

"We're all hungry."

Bernard doesn't seem to give a damn. It's strange. As if he had given up.

"You two will get through this . . ."

"Why we two? You'll get through this, too."

"Oh, I've had my life . . . I trust you, you'll make it through, with Gaëlla."

"What is wrong with you? What's got into you? Are you letting yourself go? You've got to fight. Do like me, shout!"

I tell him off. And Gaëlla gets involved, too.

"Do like Mommy, shout, make the ship come! Don't you want the ship to come?"

He had spoken about death already, before we left. As if it were something he was expecting. Is he feeling suicidal? And yet he is making plans. At times, he says:

"I'll arrange for the boat to be found and we'll set off again. I'll do what it takes to fix her up, I'll manage. Even if I have to spend the whole winter in Spain, it won't be the first time I've gone in the deep end."

And so? I no longer understand what is going through his mind. One side is positive, even though it is totally unrealistic; and the other side is negative.

"I don't care, I've had a good life, so what the hell."

I sniff the empty rum bottle. The smell is good. It only lasted two days. Two nights, mainly. Sweet and nourishing; I wanted to give some to Gaëlla, but she refused, disgusted. But she does play at putting a cigarette to her lips, pretending to smoke. Goddam carton. In the end we managed to smoke the equivalent of one pack; the rest was ruined. The bucket where he had put his bag with the cigarettes on leaving the boat keeps falling over. It irritates me.

"This fucking bucket! What's the point of having this bucket, after all? For your cigarettes, the bottle of rum and your papers? Are they so important, those papers?"

The way things stand we couldn't give a damn about his papers. The bucket falls over, the papers get wet all the time and we spend the day trying to dry them. Passport, marriage and birth certificates, identity cards, driver's licenses, address book . . .

What good is any of that right now? It keeps us busy, in any case. Dry one side, then the other, like cooking on a barbecue, and we're all happy when one page has dried out. So you say: "If I can dry this page out before counting to one thousand, we'll be rescued." Bets, like skipping steps when you're a kid, counting your steps. If I land on an even number, I win . . .

The inside pages of the address book have been spared. It is good to see something which has escaped the disaster. However small that thing might be, a few white pages.

An unending struggle between the chill of the

water immersing us and the desire to fill our bodies with water.

Water, our enemy, our providence.

We distract ourselves by spreading the banknotes out along our legs to dry them. There are pictures on them, so Gaëlla has fun. But the banknotes dry faster than anything else.

Talking is good, but it makes us thirsty, Gaëlla's orange juice is empty, and so is my bottle of fresh water. Now we're onto the survival rations. I cut open the packet with the utmost care, not to lose a drop. Gaëlla gets to drink first.

"Drink slowly, it's very precious, don't swallow it all at once, keep the water in your mouth, swish it from one side to the other so you really taste it before you swallow."

The sun is about to go down for the third time.

A quarter glass, roughly, each time. We drink it drop by drop, a ceremony of respect and precaution. Two liters of this insipid water for three people is not much. I think of all the water there was on the boat, all the water there is on earth. So much water. So much on one part of the earth, none at all on another. Out of ten packets, we'll have half left on Saturday October 8, half of that again on the 9th, then nothing. We suck at the empty packets, at an illusion of fresh water.

Airplanes fly overhead, very high, so high that we are invisible to them. People going somewhere in the world, comfortable in their seats, asking the flight attendant to bring them a drink, turning a tap to wash their hands, wasting water up there in the sky.

An obsession. What do you do when you have no more water? Wait for the rain and collect it. That's fine, but the grayish clouds above our heads are not even cottony and don't promise any rain. Filter the seawater; but with what? I know there is a system which involves putting seawater into a plate, with a plastic dome over it, and the water, as it evaporates, goes through a little tube and you can collect it, filtered. We have none of those things.

Alain Bombard maintained that it is possible to drink seawater in tiny amounts. Infinitesimal amounts. You must be psychologically prepared to do it. But what if you get diarrhea? Or vomit? Become even thirstier? The mere fact of having drunk the last drop of the last packet is already an obsession. You can't forget that last drop. It multiplies your thirst.

You can also repeat to yourself time and again, "It's not true, I'm not thirsty." But that doesn't work. The need is physical, the necessity too cruel. You know, *I* know that it is possible to remain for a long time without eating, but very little time without drinking, until you die of thirst. Not of hunger. Gaëlla is thirsty. I'm thinking about Gaëlla. I can stand anything, except for her to suffer.

So we need a cloud. Just a little cloud above our heads, to rain for us. It must be raining somewhere. Billions of clouds in the world. Just one, a little one for us.

I picture people under umbrellas, whining about

the rain which is getting them wet, and here I am begging the sky for a few drops. I pray, and pray, I spend
my time praying. I'm afraid to stop praying. I shout
my prayer to the clouds, my head raised to the stupid
dry grayness.

Gaëlla is covered with itchy spots on her behind.
It's the moisture. Your skin gets soft and flabby from
sitting in the water. Nothing ever gets dry, all our
clothing is wet, and we get these rashes where the elas-
tics of our underwear are rubbing the skin.

I clean her little round behind carefully with a
gauze strip to remove the salt on her rash. I spit on the
piece of cloth. I rub ointment over each rash. Then I
put some on her lips. She complains:

"Yuck! It's disgusting!"

"Gaëlla!"

"I don't want any, it's bad!"

"You must. Your lips will dry out and they'll hurt."

A short battle with my daughter. Just like everyday
life, basically. Children don't have the same sense of
drama as adults do. She carries on with her life, her
whims are part of it, like the Barbie dolls she asks for,
regularly, and all her questions. "Why is it all white behind the airplane? Why does it rain sometimes and
other times it doesn't?" I can answer the questions beginning with Why. Or how birds fly, how fish swim,
why the sun goes down or the wind blows. But then
there are the Will and Do questions.

"Will we still go to Grandma's? Will I have a present for my birthday? Does Daddy have a stomach
ache? Will the freighter come soon? Does God hear

us?" It takes longer and is more difficult to answer, but necessary. My daughter helps me to cope, because I am coping for her sake, above all. It's simple.

Saturday night is terrible. The sea is calmer, but still shakes the raft relentlessly. It's like a toothache you cannot stop. My improvised mattress has collapsed, I am sitting in water, I bail, I pass the sponge, I wring, I prop everything up again, I try to sleep and it starts all over.

Gaëlla is sleeping on me, and she is driest because I act as a barrier, but I am obliged so often to wake her up to stretch my legs. Cramps, pins and needles, stiff all over. She grumbles in her sleep.

When the day decides to give us light again our spirits improve a bit. The little lamp has gone out for good. The darkness is as hard to bear as the pitiful lamp which shone on us all the time. Bernard slides over on his side with difficulty, and raises the flap to look outside.

There is no light at all in the darkness. The night is dry and sinister and we have nothing left to drink. Bernard is asking for food and drink and forgiveness. He is getting delirious. He feels guilty, it's his fault, he's the one who dragged us into this nightmare. He shouldn't have abandoned ship, he shouldn't have been afraid of that goddam third wave. It probably never came. The boat is probably drifting along peacefully somewhere. Louise, are you angry with me? Oh yes, I am, but I am just as angry with myself.

I said, "Yes, Bernard. We agreed. Stop blaming yourself . . . Stop moaning, it serves no purpose."

I will always say yes. Even if it's not true. The pain in his eyes is too frightening. He has difficulty speaking, and every word is an effort. What is he going through that we are not? Hunger, thirst, cold, but what else? In vain I study the length of his body, tense with pain; I can't understand it, there is nothing visible, except for a few superficial cuts.

"Do you know how long we can last without eating? Louise, I'm so hungry, it hurts."

"Do you remember that guy who was caught in the earthquake in San Francisco, in the freeway? He lasted fifteen days, drinking his own urine."

"Do you think we should?"

"No. If it doesn't rain tomorrow, we'll try a little seawater. Just a little."

His family. His children. He begins to feel guilty about his fatherhood. A litany.

"How can I please everyone? I can't do it, Louise. I've failed my children. I'm useless. It's too late now."

"You escape, too often. Escape never solves anything. It's never too late."

This is a talk we've often had. Too much of this, not enough of the other. He has, basically, all the classical anxiety of the fifty-year old man who looks at his past. I should have, if I had . . . my son needs me, I hardly know my daughter.

"It's my fault, everything is my fault. Even with you I didn't know how."

"Okay, it's your fault. But we've had good times, we've known love, we've had a few laughs, a few adventures, and above all we have Gaëlla."

"I need you. I'm glad you're here."

"All right. But don't count on me to start over again."

"Louise? What do you have to do to be free? Shit, I wanted to be free, and I've never managed."

That wretched night was never-ending. We talked about ships, about the one that would find us. Bernard didn't want a tuna boat, they move around all the time and they're too slow. I was thinking about a cruise ship, a luxury rescue. Then he imagined a submarine. And Gaëlla, awaken by the tossing of the raft, added:

"I want a boat with a swimming pool and hot water and television, and . . . and then I want . . . first of all I have nothing to wear!"

"I'll buy you some pants!"

"I don't want pants, I want a skirt that twirls."

Thinking about her looks, my daughter. Twirling skirts, shoes, a real little starlet. A real little girl, basically.

"And I want a hot chocolate, very very very hot . . . and a sausage, a cold one, not hot, I don't like hot sausages . . . and then . . ."

Bernard dreams of an enormous steak with French fries. I dream of fruit juice, gallons of it, fountains of fresh fruit, flowing sumptuously down my throat.

Talking about food tricks our hunger and our tummies. You have to cheat your mind, tell it stories, lead it astray.

How can we cheat to be able to sleep? Water keeps leaking into the bottom of the raft and I bail and wring. Bernard blows up the rings. I would like to do it for him, because I can tell he's wearing himself out, but he refuses, vehemently. That's the only authority he has left: his power as a male, as a leader.

"It's my job to do it."

My buttocks and my feet are so cold. The sun, or warm socks, seem little more than a dream.

"I feel like a smoke."

No more matches; he's chewing on a cigarette that somehow survived, squeezing the filter between his teeth, drawing on a non-existent smoke; I do the same. I go through the motions.

"I'm fed up, Louise. I want so badly for this to end."

This is the first time he's said something like this. Up to now he has complained, felt guilty, or made crazy plans, but now he's slipping. To me it sounds like an announcement of departure.

"Stop it, be quiet."

He has frightened me. Mentally. I don't want to be drawn into this loser's attitude. To keep my mind busy I comment upon our basic equipment.

"Your bag is not even waterproof, you've been dragging your papers and your money around in a leather case—it's ridiculous!"

We've lost his foul weather jacket. A lined jacket, warm, precious. It was on the roof of the raft, drying. All our efforts to get it back by paddling towards it were in vain. Bernard is furious. Destiny is tightening its noose. I dreamt of clothespins. What a silly thing, a clothespin, and yet . . .

A little yellow notebook, tiny, with graph paper, and a plastic pen. Along with my address book that's all we have for Gaëlla to draw on to keep busy. I can't remember who first suggested making up a message. I write in French, English and Spanish, something like this: "There are three of us, including a child. We are French. We abandoned the *Jan Van Gent* on October 6, roughly 40 nautical miles from La Coruña. We are drifting westward, on a liferaft. Save us."

Bernard adds a fifty-franc note and some coins in the empty rum bottle.

Gaëlla is watching him.

"Why are you putting coins in?"

"So it makes some noise, sweetheart; and the note is the reward."

He adds a sentence to the paper. I don't know what it is, I didn't read it at the time. Probably that the actual reward will be more than fifty francs. I watch him slip the bottle into the sea. Dead calm this morning. The bottle drifts away slowly, dancing slightly at the neck. I am content. It's a positive gesture, even if it is a fragile one. I imagine a fisherman, or someone on a beach, hands picking up the glass bottle. Then immediately afterwards I imagine the bottle out at sea, ground to bits by a ship's propeller. Or shattered against a rock along the coast. It will get nowhere. Nowhere at all, ever; a message in a bottle . . . Bernard reads my mind and says dejectedly:

"It will break into a million pieces."

He lies down and closes his eyes to sleep. Or to pretend to sleep. I look for something to do, to forget the rashes which are devouring me, the grumbling in my tummy, the aches, the cramps. My address book has gotten so wet that the paper is now a pulp. I throw it out. I use a gauze strip for a calendar. I write the days of the week, the dates. In twenty days Gaëlla will be six. In twenty days we'll be at my mother's house, in France, in our family home, for a party. I'm sure of it.

Resist. Others have resisted far longer. I think of death camps, all those people you see walking along in the old photographs: their emaciated bodies, their faces so close to death. They lasted in far more terrible, horrible conditions.

"What day is it, Gaëlla?"

"You already asked me that, Mommy."

"It doesn't matter, tell me again."

"Sunday."

"Sunday the what?"

"October 9. Why do you keep asking me that same thing, over and over?"

"I'm counting how many days until your birthday."

I can't tell my little angel that we have to count the days in order to keep from going mad, to remain lucid, to have something to hold onto. We talk about the birthday, once again. The purpose of our survival. The certainty that we will be alive in twenty days. It can't be any other way. I have no idea how it will be, that's all, but we'll be somewhere near Saint-Etienne for my daughter's birthday. She'll jump up on her grandmother's neck and wear her out with questions and stories. I can hear her now:

"And then . . . you know, Grandma, and then . . . Mommy did this, and Daddy said that . . ."

She'll tell her own story of our adventure, vivacious, like all children of her age, with the words tumbling over each other, ideas running into each other. We spent a short while at my mother's this year, and Gaëlla got to know my roots, Grandma's Sicilian accent, my brothers' jokes. She put her little feet in the footsteps of my childhood. Now she knows where I come from: that her grandfather has been in heaven for a long time, that she has cousins, that her room was once mine. She left her toys there. An anchor, in a port.

Outside the weather is fine, all of a sudden. The sun. I open the flap so that Gaëlla can go to sit on the edge of the ring, her little bottom in the fresh air. Mine too, to dry out. Restore some elasticity to the skin, relieve the itching from the rash. The sun is a sign of hope. Fate has chased away the storm, the visibility has improved, and someone will see us; the day can't go by without a ship passing. I believe it, blindly. All the more so when, in this liquid desert, I see something floating. There is something, at last!

"Bernard, come and see, look!"

He emerges from his torpor, squinting in the direction I am pointing to.

"How strange. Maybe a container abandoned by a ship. Food . . . let's paddle and try to reach it."

"An orange crate. Maybe it's an orange crate, you know, people often throw oranges away when they're damaged."

As always, my dream of fruit, of liquid sugar.

It is difficult to paddle in unison on a raft like ours. The raft goes every which way, right to left, right again, like a mechanism out of synch. Bernard is stronger than I am, so his paddle forces us too far in one direction and I can't make up for it. He shouts at me.

"Keep the rhythm, do like me."

He seems better. Having a goal has given him strength. But as we draw nearer to the strange drifting object, all our hopes vanish in an instant. I give up; I'm exhausted, furious. A magma of a coal-like substance, grayish, in a pasty ball, leering at us. But a bit further away, there is something white, empty boxes or white plastic wrappers. Our paddles take up their drunken tempo once again. We pull closer. Something like seaweed is floating near the mess. Seaweed or vegetable peels, something to eat?

The flotsam is so horrible it makes us nauseous. It stinks, it's foul.

The idea that I could put something edible in my mouth had made me begin to salivate. Now I have great difficulty swallowing that saliva. Hunger, that wretched snake twisting in my stomach, is ever more present. Unbearable, in the last few minutes.

"What is it, Mommy?"

"Nothing. Garbage."

"When will we have something to eat? Can't we catch a fish? We could eat it raw, like you said, in Tahiti people eat raw fish, right Mommy, don't they?"

The fishing lines, in the fridge of the *Jan Van Gent*;

the mountain of canned food that I had so carefully inventoried, four days ago now, drifting somewhere. The last can of raviolis, that I had crossed off the list. The apples; the eggs that I had turned so carefully. A rage. Bernard breaks down.

"I've had enough, enough! Are we cursed forever, dammit? Are we jinxed? How long is it going to follow us around?"

That's what I've started to think. A jinx, bad luck, fate. Bernard should have left on his own, or with his eldest son. I showed up, and I'm the one who is on this raft. God has played a mean trick on us. I've had enough, too. But I cannot say it or let it show, that's out of the question. If I break down, Gaëlla will break down. Never. Besides, it's not in my nature.

"Shut up."

"Mommy, how is the tooth fairy going to come?"

My daughter is just like me, she talks, tells herself stories just to exist.

"I lost my tooth on Daddy's boat. The fairy will never find it, I won't have a present."

"I'll tell you how. Fairies are very clever. Wherever you are, she'll find it, and she'll bring you a present. She'll go to Grandma's when we do, and she'll see that you've lost your tooth, and bingo! she'll leave you a present on the pillow."

Gaëlla takes my breast. The moment I am no longer busy bailing, or wringing things out, or drying them, she takes refuge at my side, lifts up my T-shirt, and suckles. She is finding nourishment in my love.

We are drifting a long way, and here we are all of

a sudden under a part of the sky where it's been raining. A light mist, fine as the dew, cools our faces. I
spread the tiny particles over my drawn face; there's
not enough to drink, but the softness soothes my lips
a bit. We put our heads outside the raft and raise our
faces to this delicate moisture. The rain is farther
away, the real rain, the kind which makes things wet.
It's not for us.

Gaëlla imitates me like a little monkey. Bernard
fumes:

"It rains everywhere, except where we are!"

"Do like I do, pray to the sky, Indians pray for
rain!"

"What do you mean! Pray if you want to! If you
think there's someone up there listening to you! If
there's someone up there they're out to get us, for
sure!"

All right. You up there, if you're out to get me, well
I won't have it. You make it rain for others, and not for
me. Bernard is right. If I pray I'm accepting the cruelty
of the heavens. To plead and beg for mercy, that's
weakness. Once again I scream my anger:

"Bastard! Goddam bastard! I want land, do you
hear me? I'm sick of the sea, I've had enough! You're a
sadist, a torturer!"

I show the cross around my neck: "It's useless, absolutely useless!"

My daughter is tugging at my sleeve.

"Who are you shouting at, Mommy? Who is it?"

"God in his heaven."

"I want to shout, too. Who can I shout at?"

"What about the Holy Virgin, my angel? Go on, shout!"

Gaëlla shouts her favorite prayer:

"I want a sausage! A cold sausage! I want a ship! With a swimming pool!" Then she turns to her father: "Go on, Daddy, it's your turn! Shout what you're thinking!"

"No. I'm thinking about the boat. They found the boat at La Coruña."

Is he mad? Is he delirious?

"How do you know? Are you a seer?"

"At night I travel. I go outside of myself. I know they found it, I saw it. I know what will have to be done. I'll have to take out the engine, dry it out. There are good carpenters in Spain. It's no big deal, I can start over . . . We can leave again."

"That's out of the question. I'm staying in France, I don't want to ever go on board a boat again in my life."

I've lost all desire to shout. I suppose I have to get this poison out of me from time to time. Open a valve. My throat is dry from all the yelling. Somewhat depressed, I go back inside the damp dome. Bernard is still muttering his refrain.

"We'll find the boat, I'm sure of it. I know it. I can feel it. We'll find the boat."

"Bernard . . . we've got no more water. What are we supposed to do now? Huh?"

"We'll be rescued."

"I need to know one thing. Did you prepare a food bag?"

No. He prepared nothing. He looked for the flashlight and didn't find it. And the money, which he didn't find. I saw him go down into the saloon several times while I was getting Gaëlla ready. It was cold, we were soaked, I was looking for clothes that would be warm and easy to take with us, and for boots. He said, "I'll take care of it."

Those five words are still echoing in my mind. I don't understand. From the start I haven't been able to understand. If Gaëlla had not asked for orange juice, if I had not myself had the reflex to take a bottle of fresh water, what would have happened?

And yet he was not distraught; there was no panic. Moreover it's not like him to forget something vital on board ship. All he had to do was open the lid of the locker and take the food bag. If only he had said, "You get the food." Ever since we've been sailing together, we have had good crew reflexes: you do this, I do that, are you sure you did it? I did it.

My mistake, my big mistake, was that I did not check. I should have repeated my question before getting onto the raft. But the worst thing is that I saw him open the locker. Lean over, take something. The image is burned into my mind. This is just what I registered: he is opening the locker, he is taking the bags, he is filling the food bag.

He didn't check the liferaft. Why are there no fishing lines in a liferaft? Why so little water, why . . . why . . . It's like a pounding in my head. It's Sunday. Four days of anguish, and nothing on the horizon.

"What . . . do we do . . . now?"

It's not a question, it's a reproach, each word an accusation.

At times a mad idea comes to mind. Did he want to die? Did he do it on purpose? I'm crazy.

He takes the plastic bottle. He has diarrhea and I have nothing to help him. I turn my head, in order not to embarrass him. Gaëlla is suckling, sitting on my knees, pulling on my breast; it hurts.

I guess he is managing to wash the cut-off plastic bottle that we use for our calls of nature. I don't use it any more. It's already complicated enough to undress Gaëlla, to look after her rash.

"Mommy, the doll I had, did it stay on the boat? Or is it in Canada? Or is it in the West Indies? Or at Grandma's?"

A condensed version of the last months of our life. The doll stayed in the West Indies.

"We'll go get it, sweetheart."

"And my book. I don't even have my book so I can do my homework."

"We're going to draw flowers, on the paper."

Daisies, a house with a smoking chimney.

"I want a house made out of iron, Daddy. A house that doesn't move. Mommy, can we go camping?"

"Oh, no. No way, I've had it with camping. I want nothing to do with anything made out of canvas or cloth."

Bernard wants to talk, too. In a low voice, to spare his strength. He wants to know if I see the same colors he sees, or is he having visions. Orange here, green there, some blue. In any case I can see some smoke.

Impossible to tell how far away, but there's a cargo ship, that's for sure. Bernard puts his head out, certain that I'm seeing things, and his gaze sweeps the sea. We say nothing until the hull appears. It is moving forward, it is beige, we can see enough of it now, beige and olive green.

We think at once of the flare. A parachute flare. Bernard waits for the right moment, before it passes us and the superstructure prevents them from seeing us. Off goes the flare. We clench our teeth; it looks like the freighter is stopping. Is it stationary?

It is a terrible moment. So terrible. We have such faith. Yet at the same time we tell ourselves that the man on watch probably drank a bit too much, or that he's dozing, or that he doesn't give a damn. Maybe he's saying to himself: "No way we're going to stop and have problems." We really need a second flare, but the smoke devices aren't working.

The freighter pulls away.

A shape, laden with our wishes, our hopes, our crumbling dreams, disappearing, inexorably. I insult this phantom that is mocking us. Once again I scream:

"Stupid bastard! Idiot! Asshole! Son of a bitch!"

I insult God.

"You're not doing your job! You let any old thing happen! What are we—puppets? Do you think this is funny?"

We were so close to being saved! Beside myself, I tear the cross and chain from my neck and I throw them, a present from my mother, into the water. We go back into our shelter. Gaëlla huddles against me, giving me soft little kisses, whispering in my ear:

"Don't cry if you love me, sweet Mommy."

I wipe my tears.

The silence is orange and stinks of the rubber of our floating prison. A lasting silence. Life was so close, just there . . . It all comes back, all at once, the hunger twisting our tummies, and the thirst especially. Our entire bodies are soaked with moisture, and yet we are begging for water. Bernard stretches, closes his eyes with exhaustion, then sits up again.

"We're going to drink seawater."

This is a significant gesture, full of terrible consequence. I've thought of it sometimes while reading stories of shipwrecks, but never seriously. Today I look at the heavy, gray-green water: you can tell how salty it is, you can smell it, you can just imagine it reaching your stomach.

Bernard seems to choose his spot. He has taken the plastic cap from the rum bottle and is looking for a spot from which to scoop his dram. He chooses. I watch him, both nervous and fascinated, as he does this. He says nothing, but his hesitant arm seems to say, "No, not there . . . here perhaps? No, over there is better."

It's strange. At last he tastes it; I watch his Adam's apple rolling slowly, as if it were difficult to swallow. Then, making a face, he says,

"It's not so bad. Your turn."

He fills the cap and passes it to me. I close my

eyes, and something inside me refuses to swallow at first, then I am resigned. Gaëlla refuses with a head-shake of disgust, then gives in, too, pouting.

"That stuff makes you thirsty, Mommy."

We have taken the step. It's done. Each of us has swallowed a mouthful of seawater. Now there's nothing but to carry on with the day's usual work, sponging, bailing, wringing the clothes.

I lose a sponge. I make a desperate effort with the paddle to try and get it back, a wasted effort. I've had it, just had it. It's so sad: the freighter, gone; the sponge, gone. Our bad luck is only getting worse. Someone has put the evil eye on us, cast a spell, I'm sure of it. We have no control over events anymore. And now the sea anchor has disappeared. When did that happen? The raft is once again turning on itself and we're taking on water.

I'm so fed up. It's all so sad. We've been abandoned by everything.

Bernard changes his clothes; he washes his underwear, wringing it out, his teeth chattering. There is nothing dry left except for my T-shirt. I take it off to give it to him, and now my teeth begin to chatter. That T-shirt is the only dry thing left on earth.

"Don't do that."

He doesn't hear. He is talking about a rescue plane which will come to find us; he describes the cockpit, the pilot.

"He'll see us, don't you get it, Louise; his wings don't block the view, it's a special plane."

I think he no longer knows what he is saying. But

I can't imagine at that point that he is suffering any more from hunger, thirst, or an invisible, unknown injury than I am. I stick to a sort of reassuring logic. He's fifty, he hasn't got the same resources I have. He didn't eat for the first three days of the passage, so he's weaker, and suffers more from the cold.

I am more concerned about the seawater that we are taking on, incessantly. I'm afraid we have another leak. Waves are going over the rainwater catch and I put a bucket underneath it, but it splashes all the same. I bail, I look after Gaëlla, I cut her sweater at the elbows so it won't rub her, I put a gauze strip between her legs and tie it at her waist. I spread cream on her rashes, sparingly. Bernard has cuts along his legs so I treat them, too. Gently, with the ointment on the sleeve of my sweatshirt, to rub it with. Gently . . . I've been doing it all day. A day from hell, a day of abandonment. That freighter pulling away: the worst feeling of being abandoned. I wish I had never seen it, never known of its passage, so close.

What else? A floating buoy, made out of the bailer, which slows us down a little in our incessant waltzing. And then nightfall.

"Louise. You'll have to explain a bunch of things to Gaëlla, have to explain . . . death."

"Why?"

My daughter heard him but she doesn't understand. Death. Why death?

"Don't say that! You're going to leave me all alone!"

"Mommy, what's wrong?"

"Nothing, sweetheart."

"Daddy's proud of his little girl. You know, you mustn't get mad at me if I'm not always there with you."

"But you're there, Daddy, I can see you. I'm glad."

She crawls over to him for a delicate kiss, then comes back to cuddle up against me.

What is the matter with him? Is he giving up? Letting go? He seems to doze briefly, then talks again about a freighter finding us.

"It's the law of averages . . . a freighter has to go by . . . it's the law of averages . . ."

His eyes close once again. Then delirium. He pulls a credit card from his pocket and says,

"Here, Louise, go do some shopping."

"What are you doing, Bernard? Do you hear me? What are you saying?"

"I've had enough, go shopping, I'm hungry . . . Shit, this goddam car . . . why is it bouncing like this? I have to have a word with the salesman . . ."

All at once he starts shouting at an imaginary car salesman:

"What's the big idea, a car bouncing like this?"

I lean over his face, take his hand to calm him. He has lost weight, his beard has grown, just this afternoon, in the gray light; he looks deathly pale. He opens his eyes wide and the blue has changed to a watery green:

"I have to complain about this car, Louise."

I don't know what to say.

"Okay, I'll get up and make us a cup of coffee."

He tries to get up and go out as if he were opening a door. I realize that he thinks he is on the boat, in the wheelhouse. Quickly, I counter-attack, struggling against his delirium.

"Wait, the door is closed just now, you can't go out. I put some stuff there, you'll trip."

"No, I want to make coffee! I told you, I've had enough! This car bouncing around like this."

"Bernard, look at me! We're not in a car! Do you understand?"

No answer.

"Bernard! We're not on the boat, either. You can't make coffee."

"Why can't I make coffee? I am free to make coffee if I want. I want to drink something hot. Anyway, I'm fed up, I want to stop. Let's stop the car!"

"We're not in a car, Bernard!"

"Your driving is terrible. Watch where you're going! First right, then left, just any old way?"

He has grabbed hold of a corner of the opening flap and is hanging onto it. The raft is pitching; he's going to tip us over.

"Bernard! Be careful! You're going to make us tip over."

I'm afraid. The dialogue between us is finished, he is insistent about this car, loses his balance, blames me again for driving poorly, then yells at the salesman.

"Okay," I say, "we'll take care of it tomorrow, I'll go to see the salesman, we'll talk about it. Please, we have to get some sleep now. We must. Calm down."

Gaëlla is the one who manages to restore some calm.

"Daddy, stop, I want to sleep!"

She said the words calmly, quietly, like a mother talking to an overexcited child. And he understood. I don't know how, but there it is; he is quiet, he lies down again. Silence in the darkness.

The night of Sunday to Monday. The tossing of waves, an incessant dance: sleep, waking, then suddenly:

"It's raining!"

I heard it on the roof of the raft, a gentle rain. Quickly, I put the bucket out, and watch for it.

It must flow, the rainwater must run through, I wait for the first drop, my eyes so wide open that my lids ache. There it is, a pearl, superb. And another . . .

The glass bottle went off with our message. The cut-off plastic bottle is used for our calls of nature. There is nothing left but the bucket, but I am not going to wait for it to fill up. The cap from the rum bottle held tightly against the canvas, I fill it with these wondrous drops, one by one. Gaëlla opens her mouth, drinks . . . I drink . . . the quantity is infinitesimal, the rainwater stinks of rubber, but we are like madwomen at the sight of this water. With water you can make the world over; with water, you can save everything. The rain is continuous, and I fill up the orange juice bottle.

"Bernard, we have water, Bernard! You're going to drink!"

Still stretched out and motionless, he doesn't

reply. He hasn't realized, and yet we've been making noise, the two of us, shouting with joy. I look at his mouth, his closed eyes.

"Bernard?"

With a gauze strip I moisten his lips, which are closed and drawn over his silence; his lack of reaction still does not alarm me. Not really. Hope is there. I am going to put water into his mouth, into his body, and he will revive, say something. I moisten his face and mine. Gaëlla does the same. In the darkness, I listen to the beneficent rain, still filling the bucket, slowly. A new ritual has begun. Find the best way for the water to flow into the bottle, soak the compresses and allow us to savor mouthful upon mouthful of this fetid sweetness from heaven.

Dawn catches me at this unending task. Dampen, fill the cap, pour it into Bernard's mouth, have Gaëlla drink, then me, and begin again.

I raise Bernard's head slightly, in the pale orange glow of daybreak. He opens his eyes slightly and sees me. So I shout:

"We've got water! We're going to make it!"

His gaze is troubled, but he has understood, and is smiling, suddenly. He is happy.

It is at that moment that Bernard died. I think I didn't quite realize: that deliverance, that radiant face, so white; it was death. He was wearing his running slacks, the T-shirt I had given him, his thickish green jacket. His head was resting against the ring, his feet too, on the other side of the raft.

There is a block, suddenly, in my mind, my body,

my thoughts, my gestures; nothing left. He is dead. What am I going to do? Why did he die, first of all? I cannot comprehend that this life should suddenly stop.

During the night he was still talking, and he said to Gaëlla:

"I love you; you're the most beautiful little girl in the world."

He also said:

"I'm done for, explain to her what death is; if I die, promise me you'll have me cremated."

Cremated in this desert of water. What do you do when someone dies; I don't know.

First of all, I deny it.

"Daddy's sleeping, Gaëlla."

In my mind I go back over the number of days. Yesterday, the 10th, he was talking normally, and today, the 11th, his voice is still. It seems silly, but I cannot understand where the difference between yesterday and today lies. If I had seen him dying, if death had warned me, perhaps I would not be staring so stupidly at this body, taking half the space in the raft all by itself, inert, even larger than when he was alive.

I try to inflate the rings and it is not easy to maneuver over him. He didn't want me to do it, even yesterday he was the one who inflated the rings. This morning they are even flatter than usual, maybe because of the rain. He is dead, and I am acting as if I don't want to know. I knew it, I saw it during the night, I was even afraid that he might choke on the water, swallow his tongue, so I left him alone and devoted myself solely to collecting the rainwater. I knew, but I did not want to see. I still do not want to. The very word refuses to cross the barrier into my mind or my lips. I think, I say, "It's over." We've been hungry, we've been thirsty, now it's the end. It doesn't even hurt. It was inevitable.

His eyes are open. I thought that eyes closed by themselves at that moment. It's as if he were still looking at something.

The only thought which comes clearly to my mind is that nothing more can be expected from him, no solutions. He's not here anymore. He let me down.

"Daddy's asleep. He's going to sleep for a very long time. Don't worry. Someday we'll all meet again somewhere. Daddy is gone away, one day Mommy will go away, then it will be your turn. Everyone goes away."

She sees her father's face, his eyes wide open; I can hear myself repeating that he is asleep, that he was in pain and that he won't suffer anymore. Someone else, speaking in my place. I recite the Lord's Prayer, *Our Father, who art in heaven . . . Thy will be done . . .*

"Put your hands together, Gaëlla."

"Why do we have to do this?"

"We have to say a prayer to thank the heavens for the rain, and to see Bernard on his way. We mustn't be sad, he would see it if we were sad. He mustn't feel bad, do you understand?"

What stupid things am I saying. What stupid things am I thinking. Bernard, you're going to help us now that you are up there. You're going to make a freighter change course and send it to us. Do it, for your daughter.

She doesn't cry. She is calm. I'm the one who is losing ground, slowly, in silence. I wonder what kind of scenario I'm in. Whether we are living or dead. Where are we? In what universe? What am I supposed to do? What is my role in the story? If Gaëlla asked me questions, it might be easier.

I pick up a jacket and fold it to make it into a mattress. I don't know how many times I say to her, "Daddy's sleeping."

At one point Gaëlla says something which causes me to start.

"Look, he's moving."

His body is moving with the motion of the raft. He is sleeping. I can't tell how the day is going by. I feel I am waiting for him to wake up. And I think, too, of this strange coincidence which caused the rain to come at the same time as his death. Deliverance. For him, from suffering; for us, that we might drink. Now the freighter will come. He will have a decent funeral, a ceremony. Now we've reached the end of the story. There cannot be anything worse.

I even think he has died to set us free. There. We loved, we ceased loving, he was there, he is no longer there.

CHAPTER FOUR

The Days

W E HAVE REACHED the depths of horror.
Gaëlla is curled up against me and we
are trying to keep as far away as possible
from the body. I am afraid the raft will tilt and that he
will fall upon us. The water is icy, the air is icy. My
mind has great difficulty in accepting what has happened to us. Up until now things were relatively easy
to explain: the storm, hunger, thirst, drifting, anxiety—
but not death. I have never seen a dead person before.
I understand nothing.

I inflate the rings, making superhuman efforts not
to fall onto him. At times I place my hand on him, to
touch him, perhaps to try and realize, as if I were waiting for him to wake up. This deep final sleep, his silence, horrify me.

We almost never stopped talking. We had to talk,
to stifle fear, to keep our brains working. All those sentences we said, all the memories, reproaches, com-

ments, have left with him. I would like to remember them, word for word, talk again about life, find what went wrong. I dropped a stitch in the knitting.

I no longer count the days—the 11th, or the 12th—I no longer cross them off on the gauze strip calendar. This must be what is called an emotional shock. If someone were to ask me what I felt, I would be incapable of describing it in any other way than by saying: "I just didn't understand."

It was on the 13th that I got such a fright. His feet were blue, his body soft to the touch. Suddenly I thought he was going to empty himself and that it would be awful. The only thing I knew about death was that a body empties itself afterwards.

I wanted to close his eyes, and I didn't know how. I thought it would be enough to place my fingers on his eyelids for them to close on their own, like in the movies. My symbolic gesture did nothing. I was confused. I had to force them shut. His eyelids closed, then opened again. As if he were looking at me, leering. He couldn't stay there any longer, I could wait no longer. Suddenly, a violent urge to clean the space of our lives took hold of my brain. An obsession. To live without that body.

I had to get him into the water, and explain to my daughter why. I did so, gently.

"Gaëlla, the freighter is not coming, there's no one to help us, and when a sailor dies you have to put him into the water, that's the way it is. It's safer. So I'm going to put Daddy in the water. Do you understand?

Three days and two nights. I've kept him as long as possible, but now we must."

"If you have to, then do it, Mommy."

"If you have another solution, another idea, then tell me, Gaëlla."

As if my daughter could help me, encourage me. As if she were an adult. I need her approval to get on with this job. I coax myself in silence. You're going to take him and tip him over the edge.

It took me all afternoon to get it done. You don't just take a body as if it were a bag and tip it over the edge, simple as that, oh no. First of all you recoil, you're terrified to actually touch the body. I was going crazy. Because there were clothes it was still possible, just a rapid gesture. But to grasp him round the torso—that I couldn't do.

To take him by the ankles was beyond my mental capacities. His ankles were bare and his skin frightened me. So I tried to take him by the calves so that the cloth would protect me from the terrifying contact.

"Gaëlla, sweetheart, you must give Mommy some strength, some courage."

"I love you, Mommy, very very much."

"You might have to help me push."

"Oh no, Mommy, I can't . . . I can't help you."

Move my legs, sit down, breathe out, breathe in, look outside, and begin again. He is on one side, I'm on the other. I force myself, unthinking, to grasp his legs, pull a bit, and take a breath. Keep my balance, maintain stability with each movement. I have no more strength. My arms refuse to make the effort. The raft moves around so much: how can I have a hold? I'm struggling against so many things at the same time, inertia, fear, the rolling of the raft.

I stop, realizing that his weight is balancing the raft. The moment I tip him off the edge, if I manage to, there's a risk we'll capsize. And yet I absolutely must do it. Absolutely.

I begin tugging on his legs again, in vain. I talk to my daughter to give myself some courage.

"How can I do it, Gaëlla? What do you think? How?"

"Well. Try another way. If you can't do it with his feet, try some other way."

Poor baby. What sort of perverse destiny has decided to inflict this nightmarish situation on my little girl. It's her father who lies there, cumbersome, terrifying, the father who loved her and whom she loved. She would dance for him, she would laugh, throw herself into his arms, and now here I am asking her what I should do to get rid of him. My brain is made of concrete, I'm going mad. I must act; action is the only thing that will save me from this madness hanging over me.

I try once again to raise his torso, and that doesn't work either. He is now in a sitting position, and it is even more terrifying.

"Gaëlla, shout with me, shout!"

She calls weakly, "Go on, Mommy," and I shout so that she will shout.

"Louder! Help Mommy! Shout louder! We have to do it today."

The light is fading; I refuse to spend another night with him on board. I refuse. Gaëlla shouts, "Go on, Mommy, go on! I love you, you can do it!"

"Think about Daddy, Gaëlla. Think about him, it will be good for him."

What madness, this disjointed dialogue, this intense panic which just won't give me the necessary rage. I have managed to swing him round and pass his feet through the opening of the raft. It's already better but I'm still no further ahead. I have to tip him off the edge. One way or another. I'm back to square one, really.

I take a long time to catch my breath, maybe half an hour. I talk to him, I ask him to help me; he's the dead one, can't he do something, give me an idea. And suddenly, it comes. The positive rage which surges at last, which makes me take a jacket and pass it under Bernard's waist, knot it by the sleeves, so that I manage to lift him at last. A victory.

Gaëlla is still shouting to encourage me. I have found the maneuver; like this I won't have to touch his body, and the jacket will give me a hold. Until the moment when I realize I will still have to use my hands. If I don't, there's a risk I too might fall in the water, and the vision of Gaëlla all alone on the raft acts as a stimulus. I see myself swimming, her screaming, the raft drifting away, the separation, the loss.

"Help me, Bernard, for heaven's sake!"

I am angry with the entire world. With God, with the land, with the sky, I curse the universe, until at last the body falls into the water and I recoil, terrified and breathless, my arms outstretched to keep my balance.

I watch as the body turns over onto its back, as if he had decided to be in that position forever with his arms crossed over his stomach.

"Gaëlla, do you want to watch Daddy going away?"

"No."

He is wearing his yellow foulies; someone might see him. A freighter might locate him, go round in circles, and come to get us.

She didn't want to keep anything of his, not even the ring I gave him. Not even a piece of clothing.

We were vagabonds together, the two of us. The sea brought us together, and now it has separated us.

I am trembling with exhaustion. With cold. With relief. Gaëlla is in her corner. I have to make her walk, move around to keep the blood circulating. I have to bail, inflate, wring. I have work on board this fucking orange raft. My bum hurts, I have rashes everywhere, my stomach is a hellhole of cramps. Gaëlla, who was constantly asking for food, has become a bit calmer since Bernard left. The leitmotif seems to occur less often. A weaker refrain.

"I want to eat. I want a freighter."

If only I could fish. A hideous fish showed up and it has been obstinately following us for a while; we would gladly devour it raw. If I could make a hook. There is the hoop which hangs from a lanyard to be used to right the raft if it capsizes; but that's the problem, what if I make a fish hook with it and then we capsize? What about the bucket, then? Careful,

Louise, what if you fall. If only . . . Always *if*, I have no other language than if.

That fish is irritating me. It has been there since I put Bernard in the water. It is swallowing the crumbs of tobacco I mopped up with the water. A ridiculous fish; it is ugly, gray, with globular eyes.

"Gaëlla, say hello to the fish."

"What are we going to do now, Mommy?"

"I'm going to teach you things by heart."

"What for?"

"So that you can learn them . . . go on, answer, where does Grandma live?"

"Near the school."

"Where is the school?"

"Well, next to Grandma's house."

I'll have to do better; her childish logic has caught me unawares. I'll start with the town, the street, the number of the house. At times it annoys her but I stick with it.

The rubber bottom of the raft ripples; I feel a presence.

"What is it, Mommy?"

"Ssh . . ."

It's a shark, or sharks. It's rubbing its back, just beneath us. It could flip us over with one wiggle of its back.

"What is it?"

I force her to be quiet. Without using the word "shark", which might frighten her. All my senses on the alert, I observe the threatening movement, silently praying. Don't let us be eaten by sharks, my God, I beg of you . . . Silent, we sit huddled together. God is listening to me: there is a nervous, aggressive rippling beneath my legs, one last thrust, then nothing. Gone. But for a long time I lie listening with my entire body, Gaëlla stretched out on top of me.

Now I must think of the rain, too strong, and the roof of the raft which is getting softer, and the bottom which is getting even more soaked. Great quantities of seawater are coming in through the flap. The improvised sea anchor is no longer there, chewed off by the shark. The awful fish is gone, too. It must have followed us for three, four or five days. It must be . . . October 15.

It was the 15th, but from that day on I lost all notion of time. An hour is as long as a day. I made a doll out of a gauze strip, drew her eyes and mouth. We play tea party to trick our hunger. We have to talk about food to forget it. Talk about it until we're nauseous.

My father had a vegetable garden. He grew peas, carrots, lettuce, tomatoes, leeks. He also raised hens and ducks, and a pig. His motto was, "Eat healthy food." He was a peasant in Sicily before he became a worker in France, and he really only knew the land, the security it gave. What he had grown and raised could be found in a big cupboard filled with supplies; in case of emergency, if you wanted to eat, all you had to do was open that cupboard door. We never wanted for anything. He would buy an entire calf or a sheep and then cut it up to put it in the freezer. He made sausages, blood pudding. My mother made pasta with every imaginable sauce.

I tell Gaëlla about my childhood meals. We make up menus. Sausages, hot chocolate, steak and French fries, oranges, raviolis in tomato sauce.

"Draw a pork chop for me."

We can last a long time drinking rain water, that I know. My resistance is good, too, perhaps better than average. My peasant origins, no doubt. The hard land of my Sicilian ancestors.

"Mommy, where does the moon go? Why are we small? Why do we grow up? Why are there men and women? Mommy, why do we have babies in our tummies and not our backs?"

She will be married in a white dress, to have a baby. I will find a daddy, to make a little sister, that way she'll have someone to play dolls with. The best would be a daddy who is a grocer or a baker, who would give her cakes and chocolate eggs with toys inside.

"You know, you mustn't choose someone just for what you want. The main thing is to love him."

"Why do we love people, Mommy? Why are there some we don't love?"

We talk continuously about the whys. The horizon is still empty. This morning I saw a bird, very high in the sky. Maybe the land is near. The land, full of grocery stores and restaurants and supermarkets and bakeries. Talking about food is like negotiating with one's hunger. Tricking it. You know you're hungry, the cramp is there, but you manage to live with it. Just knowing there are human beings who have lasted fifteen days or three weeks in atrocious conditions: if they lasted, so can we. You drink something to ease the spasms. You can feel your stomach shrinking. We have drunk so much water that my stomach is bloated. Gaëlla had diarrhea, and that frightened me, but it's stopped now.

"Mommy, my wee-wee is really clear."

Another little victory. The rainwater has saved us, for the moment. In the end we drank very little seawater. I did a lot of house cleaning one day when it was pouring. There were still those damned brownish crumbs of tobacco everywhere. I am careful to keep the bottle constantly filled, just in case the bucket tips over.

Bernard is sleeping somewhere, on the water. I talk to the sea. I tell it that it has hurt me so much that I hate it. I think about my mother. Does she know we have disappeared? If they found the boat afloat, she knows. She could not understand how I could leave with Bernard.

"How can you go off with a man you've divorced?"

She didn't like him. He had drawn me into an adventurous and unstable lifestyle. He had hurt me. She couldn't understand that we remained friends all the same. Bernard was, once and for all, her only daughter's bad genie. When it's time for me to face her, he will stand guilty for having dragged Gaëlla and me into this terrible adventure. I will also stand guilty for having followed him. I am angry with myself. I am angry with him. But he is dead.

What is the point of being angry with someone who is dead? In the end I refuse both my guilt and his.

The guilt lies with fate, or God, the sea, the land which abandoned us, the ships which have not passed our way.

"Mommy, do you think God has punished me because I didn't always finish my plate? I'll always finish it from now on."

She is fussy about food. Cleaning her plate—that has often been our little daily battle.

"Why is there no ship?"

She doesn't scream, doesn't cry; just a plaintive little voice, wanting something when she can't understand what's happening to her. Whose fault, my God, how can it be my fault? Impossible. I left with her father, precisely for her sake, so that they could be together and share their love.

"We'll get out of this. We have to be patient, that's all. When you believe in something hard enough, it happens."

The ship that will come will have a beautiful swimming pool. We sing. Gaëlla adores Patrick Bruel. *Casser la voix*. She used to sing it with her father, who would clown around, imitating the singer hanging from his microphone, At times I wondered who was the more childish of the two. He used to take her for piggyback rides and they would laugh themselves silly.

The last picture of tenderness remains carved in my memory. He was in pain and couldn't move, so she crawled over to him to give him a kiss and said, "I love you, my Daddy."

"Mommy, you're the most beautiful mommy."

She is caressing my face; she needs to be on top of

me, to touch me all the time, because my protection, my breast, are vital. Sometimes I can't even sleep.

On land she never used to leave me either. Often she wanted to sleep with me; I should have refused but I always gave in. Bernard often said, "You overdo it, she's forever in your skirts, she clings too much. You have to make her more independent."

Overdo it? What is overdoing it? The simple fact of looking at her, letting my gaze settle on her, gives me the feeling I am protecting her and giving her everything. I look at her in the way my mother looked at me, she looks at me as I looked at my mother, the umbilical cord has never been cut among the three of us, it is a silent thing, indestructible, and it needs no words in order to exist. To take a hand, to kiss, touch, caress—we all need physical contact, warmth, gazes. It's an animal thing.

"How many brothers does Mommy have?" I ask.

She lists them: Michel, Paul, Mario and Angelo. Grandma lives in a country called France, in a little village which is called . . . the postal code is . . . the phone number is . . . One day Grandma gave me a little goat.

"Could I have one? When we get back on land we'll live with animals. We'll go to Grandma's; she knows how to do everything, Grandma does, lots of cooking too."

"Get up, Gaëlla, I have to see if there is a ship."

"No, Mommy, I don't want to . . . I want to stay like this, it's nice."

The little hole is still there between the first and

the second ring; there is a leak. What if the rain submerges the raft, what if the roof is no longer waterproof . . . Could I make fishing lines with the zippers from our jackets?

My feet are so swollen I can't get them into my boots. I have to use Bernard's. It's all that's left of him.

"Let's cook some rice. We need a saucepan, some water, and salt . . . And if we made some pancakes?"

"Be careful, Gaëlla, your pancake has flipped up to the ceiling!"

Today we're going into a supermarket to steal everything we feel like eating. We can't go during the day, of course, so we'll go at night. We'll hide in the clothing department until everyone's gone, and then, where shall we begin?

"First yogurts and cream cheese, then sausages."

"Wait, don't go so fast, begin at the beginning. You open the yogurt."

She opens it, eats, licks the spoon, then takes a swig of fruit juice.

Food, snacks, anything edible, an obsession.

She is so good at pretending to eat; I admire her. On land she would stamp her foot, she was so fussy; here she puts up with the situation better than an adult would.

"Do you want some cake?"

"Yeah!"

"Don't say yeah, Gaëlla, say yes . . ."

Nothing is happening. Yesterday we saw a rainbow and Gaëlla made a wish. So did I. I said, "I wish this would end."

And she said, "I wish I could have a sausage."

She is sleeping in her foul weather jacket, with the hood; I put a plastic bag on my head. My perspiration and breathing keep up a sort of warmth inside the bag.

And you, up there, Bernard: you're not doing much to help us. What the hell are you doing? You don't answer. I'm going to ask my grandmother. She had the gift of healing, her name was Louise, like me.

"Listen, Grandmother, there are only two possibilities left. Either a freighter goes by and doesn't see us, and it's all over for us, forget it, or it goes by fifteen feet away and it has to see us. So go on, do something."

I have spoken to everyone I know, even people I don't know. Jeannie Longo, for example, who shares my last name; an extraordinary sportswoman. I said to her, "We'll show them that Longos are tough women. Longos are strong . . ."

A slogan for my daughter, Longos are strong . . .

I have stopped marking the passage of days on the rag doll's apron. Night and day have become drowned in the same fetid water, the same rotting dampness. I have taught Gaëlla how to fill the bottle, how to inflate the three valves, how to bail. She hardly wants to move anymore. I don't actually realize how exhausted she is. I mustn't.

Survive, hang on, keep one's brain working, stay free of delirium. The aim is to hang on. Longos are strong . . .

We have been gliding through these phantom days, all identical, on a flat ocean. But the swell has risen. A long swell. Outside, the sky is beautiful. In the northwest, fine white filaments of cloud announce the coming of wind.

I blow up the rings as tight as they'll go, emptying my lungs. One of the valves is identical to the nozzle of the pump. A curse on whoever thought up anything so stupid. If he were here, the idiot . . .

The raft is sturdy, all the same, even though it is getting worn. Night is coming, I can feel the weather changing. Strong wind somewhere. I pray it doesn't come our way.

"Are you okay, Mommy?"

"Yeah, I'm okay."

"Don't say yeah, Mommy, say yes."

We have to sleep. My head in the plastic bag, Gaëlla bundled up in her foulie, with the hood pulled down. We have to sleep, to hang on. To dream.

I dreamt of a farm with a large orchard and lots of animals. I saw myself in the sun, like some organic farmer, with goats, cheese, bouquets of flowers, baskets of fruit and vegetables. Gaëlla was running in the grass. There were trees, land. It was solid, beneath our feet. I was standing. That's what land is, it doesn't move, and you can stand on it.

I have slept. Gaëlla curled up beside me. The same leaden sleep.

It was the last night. My daughter's last night. I thought I had reached the limits of horror, that I had been subjected to inconceivable punishment, but we were alive, and I had lost neither hope nor strength, nor my trust in "something." I had recited the Lord's Prayer as often as I had insulted the heavens. I had dreamt up all the possible solutions, used my intelligence to the limits of its strength. I had managed not to panic. Bernard was dead. I had forgotten him out of vital necessity. I had tidied things up in my mind and on the raft. But the sea had not finished tidying things up with me.

The freighter came upon us in the morning, brutally, while we were still fast asleep.

A monster.

CHAPTER FIVE

The End

A T FIRST I don't understand what's happening to us; the raft has spun round, three hundred and sixty degrees, and there before me, twelve or fifteen feet away, I see a brick-colored hull. A wall of metal with enormous propellers. I wave my arms, shouting like a madwoman: "We've won! Gaëlla, we've won! Look!"

It turns around, the hull passes us, closer, to get into a position to pick us up. I think immediately of the rope ladder we will have to climb. I pull off my boots, to be more agile.

Gaëlla seems fine. She has even made a joke, which surprises me:

"Is that the ship? I wanted an ocean liner!"

The sea is fairly choppy, but the sky is blue and the visibility is excellent. The ship is called the *Petrovski*.

I wonder what language I'll be able to speak.

Spanish, French, or English? The ship is moving on, under its own momentum, and I know it will take some time before it can swing round. I'm not at all worried. It's finished, finished; the nightmare is finished.

Now it is coming back, slowly steaming ahead. I am on its port side and I can hear the muted rumbling of the engines. I had thought it was a huge ship, surprised by the closeness of the hull, but I can see it is actually fairly small.

I help Gaëlla remove her boots, we put on our lifejackets, and I explain to her that we are surely going to have to climb up separately.

"They're going to drop a rope ladder, we'll help you, don't be scared."

It seems so long. The freighter goes by the raft again, a bit further away so that its wake does not cause us to rock over. Leaning out the opening I can see a sailor on the bridge throwing a lifebelt overboard. Just a ring buoy, without a rope to the ship: what's the point? It's idiotic. I grumble, "Stupid idiot."

But I catch the buoy anyway, even if it's useless. The swell is rising, the *Petrovski* has cut its engines and is coming nearer. I cannot make out what flag it's flying. So I shout, confusedly, "Throw a line! A rope! *Corde! Ligna!*"

I can't stop moving. Bernard used to say, "If you see a freighter, show them that you're alive." I wave my arms, I shout, I put my head back in to talk to my daughter, I stick it out again like a jack in the box, I wait hopefully for a rope, for the rope ladder, I'm in a hurry to have Gaëlla grasp onto something, to tear her from this raft; I can already picture her up on the deck, and see myself climbing behind her.

I don't understand what they're doing. A sailor in a wet suit is in the process of sliding down the rope, as fast as he can, to splash in the water before my very nose. I don't notice that he has let go of the rope. As I help him to climb onto the liferaft I pray to heaven that the sea won't throw us against the steel hull. He climbs aboard with some difficulty and begins speaking English with a terrible accent. He places his hand on my head as if to reassure me.

"I've won!"

He doesn't seem to understand.

"I've won, the birthday, on October 29 . . . it's the 22nd today, I've won."

The poor fellow doesn't understand that I've been obsessed by the idea of Gaëlla's birthday. I had promised myself that we would spend it at my mother's house. By October 29 it would be all over. So I've won, that's obvious, but how can he know any of that? He looks at me with big round eyes, patting me on the head.

"It is the 20th of October . . ."

"We'll go to Grandma's, I've won!"

October 20? There are two days missing in my head. I look at our rescuer, impatiently, annoyed. I explain in broken English that I have lost my husband, that we are French; I tell him the name of the sailboat. And he repeats that everything will be fine and that I'll be able to rest.

He is relatively young, thirty or forty, thin, strong and fairly tall. He is so kind to Gaëlla; he was surprised to find her there. They must have thought I was alone. He says he is Russian; we have some difficulty understanding each other.

"Gaëlla, put your boots on, put your boots on, I don't want you to scrape your feet when you climb up."

I have to put them on her myself, and bail, but she pulls them off again.

"Gaëlla, help Mommy."

She refuses. And yet she is happy, at that moment. She is smiling.

The raft, suddenly heavy with the weight of the sailor, is taking on water again; he is bailing, shouting words I don't understand in the direction of the hull. There is indeed a ladder against the hull, but it is fixed and only comes halfway down, impossible to reach. The swell has caused us to spin off to one side and we are paddling to try to come closer. They toss him a line, he manages to catch it, but it's a struggle to try and attach us; he doesn't manage and has to let go. Between the movement of the freighter and the swell, it's impossible. I begin to see it's not going to be as easy as I had thought. When this man dropped so easily from his rope I thought it would be just as simple for us. Not at all the case. He repeats: "We'll manage." But every maneuver the ship makes is incredibly slow, and as soon as it gets closer to us it has to stop its propellers. Finally I grab hold of a line with a big knot at the end. I am so happy to have succeeded that it takes me a few minutes to realize that if I don't let go it's going to pull my arm off. The freighter tries to reposition itself, time is wasting, it takes forever, forever, and the sea is getting rougher, it's dangerous. I'm getting annoyed.

More than once I manage to catch the rope, only to let go again. The sea is too rough, there is no way I can do this maneuver. I expected a rope with a harness, for the fellow to tie Gaëlla and hoist her up.

They should jettison some fuel onto the water to calm the sea. Why hasn't the captain thought of this? I shout at him to do that, but no one up on deck understands me. Then I think of a crane. A freighter has to have a crane, to load its cargo. I tell my rescuer:

"The crane . . . use the crane . . ."

"No, it's okay . . . no problem . . ."

At one point I yell at him in French: "Take the paddle, dammit!"

Yet the poor guy is trying. When he got here, I felt that at last I would be taken care of, there was someone alive, a strong man, he was going to fix everything. But this bitch of a sea just won't let us, it just won't let us.

"Bitch, can't you stop for just a moment? Just a tiny bit, a little tiny bit . . ."

Now I am frightened. These people don't really seem to know what to do. There must be a certain technique to rescue operations. Since they can't drop a whaleboat, they should think of how to hoist us with their crane. I can't stop shouting at the crew with my fist raised.

I no longer understand what they're playing at. Figures, bundled up, stare at us from the deck without being able to do a single thing. It's terrible, we can see life so close and yet we still can't reach it. At one point the raft drifts dangerously close to the hull, I could reach out and touch it; the freighter wavers and almost crushes us, I just have time to put my hands on Gaëlla's head to get her to duck down quickly.

The raft rubbed against the steel hull, covered with barnacles and studded with huge bolts. I hope the raft has not been torn. Not now! It has to hold on a bit longer. The opening gives onto the waves running along the side of the hull. Suddenly I cry, "Watch out!"

It's useless, and too late. The raft flips over. Usually it rights itself fairly easily, but for the first time it remains tipped over. Here we are, sitting on the roof, our feet in the water. I am holding onto Gaëlla, she is clinging to me, her little legs seeking out a place to lodge against mine. It's not easy because my feet are pressing against the hoop which is supposed to support the roof like a tent. The water is up to my chest and I have to keep my balance like a floater.

The sailor manages to get out of the upturned bubble. The water is not all that cold; I thought it would be worse.

We cling onto the straps. There is very little space left to breathe, between the surface of the water and the canvas. You have to put your head to one side to get air. Gaëlla says nothing. I'm the one who's shouting.

I can hear some scraping noises above us. I hope

the sailor is going to right the raft, and quickly; no, instead of that he climbs on top of it! We try to talk through the canvas. I want him to get off there, he has a wetsuit on, he can hang on and swim around, but we can't.

I want him to help me right the raft, but he refuses, and just goes on saying that everything will be fine, that I mustn't worry!

I don't know what's going on outside now. I just have to trust him. But Gaëlla is having a hard time keeping her balance and she won't be able to hold on like that for long. I can also see that we lost everything when we capsized; there is nothing left to bail with if the fellow does manage to get us upright again.

Time goes by. The dialogue continues, broken, surrealist. In English or in Spanish; I use all the words that come to mind. Then suddenly a silence. He doesn't answer. I ask:

"Are you there? Is someone there?"

The horror of it—he's not there anymore, the bottom of the raft above my head is soft. He let go. He left.

"Gaëlla, listen to Mommy, we're going to do like at Eurodisney, do you remember? Mommy's going to turn the raft over . . . Hold on tight . . ."

She doesn't answer, but I manage the maneuver without any problem. My foul weather jacket is gone, my boots, the bottle, nothing left but the scarf around my neck, my jacket, nothing left to bail with, and we're taking on water.

I am furious, on the verge of hysteria, shouting at

the freighter. There is no way I will let this one get away, I'll go to the limits of my strength but I won't let go! It pulls away, returns, pulls away again, I still can't figure out what it is doing. I remember the story of that Greek freighter where they tossed the stowaway immigrants into the sea. Who is on board this one? Rescuers or assassins?

They must have realized they would not be able to pick us up and they would rather slip off and leave us there—could that be it? They must be thinking: "They'll just die, and no one will ever know . . ."

I shout at God, I shout at Bernard. I call him an idiot.

"You've got it easy up there. You don't risk a thing now. Can't you help us a bit?"

Gaëlla is still silent. She has no strength left; the time in the water, clinging to the straps, balancing on my legs, was really too much for her. Her face is quite pale, and her enormous eyes are a dreadful reproach. I talk and talk, reassuring her, trying to paddle, to follow the freighter, getting nowhere. I raise the flap to make it into a sail; I'm going mad, insane. How could it have failed—we were so close! Impossible!

The raft is once again by the hull, I can see the men on deck, I don't know what they're doing, but they have been busy, without paying any attention to me, so it seems. I no longer exist, they don't give a damn! I shout my lungs out:

"*Yo tengo una niña!* I got a baby! *J'ai un enfant! Un enfant!* Baby!"

The enormous shape in front of me, the rising sea,

tossing me close to the propeller. Will it ever end? I insult the sea, tell it to calm down, but it doesn't care. I insult the freighter, and it doesn't care either; it is leaving, clearing out, the bastard!

"If you let me down, if you just leave like that, without doing a thing, you'll remember me! I swear it!"

And now comes the most awful moment of my life. I don't know what's going on, on board the freighter; nobody has told me a thing. They've just abandoned me, without a word, or a hope, and, as I turn back to my daughter I notice for the first time since our struggle together on the raft began that there is something wrong.

I've lost my foulies, I'm very cold, I must be trembling, but the only thing which makes me sick with anger is that I have nothing left to shelter her with. She can't lie down on the bottom any more, there's too much water, she is standing up, a tiny, stiff body, hanging to the straps, with her back to me.

Her hands are gripping so tightly to keep from falling that I have difficulty freeing them. I want to hold her close to me.

"Turn around, sweetheart . . . Come to Mommy . . ."

My daughter is stiff as a board. Her eyes are wide open, staring, her long lashes sticking to her cheeks. It's as if she has frozen herself into this position by a superhuman effort of will.

As I turn her face toward me I see drool on her lips. I draw her to me, she doesn't react. I call her, my head in her soaking, salty hair.

"Gaëlla . . . it's Mommy . . . sweetheart . . . I'm going to sit you down, Mommy has to see where the freighter has gone."

The time to look through the flap, to see that goddam ship sailing away toward the horizon, disappearing in the swell; the time of nothingness. A few seconds. My little girl has slumped into the water, stretched out on the bottom of the raft, she is floating, her eyes staring ahead; she isn't fighting anymore. It's over. Like Bernard. All at once, before I had time to see death arrive.

Maybe I am screaming, but maybe I'm not. The shock is too sudden, the evidence too violent. It seems I am thinking about her father, that I am angry with him for taking her from me. She is leaving with him. I see myself pick her up, growing desperate, losing it. Why now, just like that, all of a sudden?

I don't know what to do. I try mouth to mouth, but I don't manage to bring her back. I know, anyway, that she is no longer alive. I know it. And I cannot stand this face in the water, these eyes full of water. It's beyond anything I can accept.

Later I was told that the freighter found us at 8:30 A.M.; I don't know what time it left us, it felt like the afternoon to me, and in fact it was about one o'clock. We must have tried for five or six hours. But I didn't realize.

I tried, I fought so hard, so long, the hours no longer make any sense. All I know is that the sea is empty, we've been abandoned, and Gaëlla is gone. It's the end of this horrid, insane story. The end.

✳ 116 ✳

I am alone. Alive, there before her, and I cannot stand it. The faces of my loved ones parade through my mind. My mother, my brothers; I fought to bring her back to them, I fought for her sake, because of her. Without my daughter perhaps I would not have made it. She was my treasure, my life. I'm going to die. I'm going to drown in this cursed water. I tell myself, so simply, "I'm going to kill myself."

I will lower my daughter into the water so she can join her father. I cannot stay here looking at her afloat in the water; her drowned eyes will drive me mad.

I lived with Bernard's body for three days. But my daughter's is sheer horror, pure despair. It's more than I can bear, and I no longer know what I am doing. And yet every gesture of that time is burned into my memory.

I am going to remove my lifejacket and kill myself. I'll simply sink, like a stone.

Some imbecilic journalist will ask me, later, "But how did you plan to commit suicide?"

It's not the type of question you ask yourself at the time. In fact you don't ask any more questions at all. It's like a film, a succession of images coming through your mind. Feet first or not? Shall I let myself slide? I'm not going to swim, I'm not going to do anything. The water is going to numb me. The water of the wave—I can still see it, that wave, passing through my mind. But this time, I'll be the one to decide. I am going to sink, very logically, I can see myself doing it.

I am going to remove my lifejacket because you cannot sink with a lifejacket. That is what I thought, very clearly. As for the rest, I would drop straight down, and I would not suffer. It was all that there was left to do. I was talking to Gaëlla, too.

"You were conceived on the water, you have returned to the water."

And to the freighter.

"We were fine, the two of us; why did you come here? We could have lasted longer, what did you do to us, bloody fool?"

I could not know that the freighter left solely because the sea was too rough and they were afraid of crushing us. I did not think for a second that they might be calling for a helicopter. I did not even know how far from the coast we were. Or even that they might be waiting for the swell to subside before they would come back. None of that.

I had to get Gaëlla into the water, some sort of funeral ceremony, and then kill myself, because my life was over. And yet my mother was still there in my mind: she was the only one holding me back at the edge of the liquid abyss. She would never know what had happened to us, I thought. Something shifted inside me, a tiny positive thought.

I thought about her again, as I left Gaëlla to the sea. I knew my mother would not understand my gesture. But I had to do it. I wanted to do it, I did it, and at the same time I felt guilty for parting from her body. The fact that I could not bear to see it. That I needed to get rid of everything, everything. Including myself. Everything into the sea.

"It's what you want, wretched ocean. I won't fight

anymore. There's no reason to fight, you've won, you've won."

I was cut off from the living world. I had accepted reality.

I could see what I was doing, I thought I was lucid. And, in my opinion, I was. Completely lucid. I could never have stood the idea of a grave. The land could go and fuck itself.

I was so far gone that the land could explode. And yet I was angry. It is probably my anger which made me the sole survivor. That is probably what people could not forgive. And so many other reactions on my part.

I am, in some way, an indestructible animal. Who knows why.

I was about to remove my lifejacket when a red flare burst on my right. The noise made me start. I stopped where I was, in mid-gesture, dumbfounded; I looked up to see what was happening and saw an airplane. An airplane! I hurled more abuse at them:

"Bloody stupid bastard! What can you do? Do you expect to land on the sea?"

In fact the plane was spraying a fluorescent liquid to mark the raft's position.

And now the helicopter is arriving. I can see it. Stupefying, this roaring helicopter. Whirling in the sky.

At that moment, I tip off the edge, but on the side of life. I want to live. I want to show that I am alive, that I am here, moving, that I am fed up; I shout something, God knows what, at the helicopter. It is taking too long, whirling up there, forty or fifty feet away; what the hell are they doing? In fact they were calculating my drift in the wind to find their position, but I could no longer think logically. My anger would not leave me. Insults, that was all.

Then I realize that someone is sliding down the rope. I can see a red suit, arms holding something, equipment. The man is now only six feet away, then in the water, it's not easy, he is struggling, then I manage to grab a hand and pull, putting my weight to one side so he can climb onto the raft. At last he is there, talking. At first I cannot understand what he is asking, in Spanish, then at last I answer:

"I don't have a daughter."

He doesn't insist. He has some gear in a yellow box, a coil of rope.

It all happens quickly, this time. He makes it clear to me that we have to proceed very rapidly.

"We'll go back up."

He passes a harness to me and mimes the movement I will have to make in order not to stay too close to him. I understand, I obey, I am so fed up. I am so cold.

I don't know how long the rescue lasted. I was tired and couldn't take any more. I saw the fluorescent liquid, I was not dizzy, and when I arrived in the fuselage I nearly passed out. The men lifted me inside and I lay on the floor. Three men: the pilot, the co-pilot and the rescuer.

They took my lifejacket off. Hands removed the

gauze strips I had wound around my legs. Cold. Sick of my sodden clothing. My underwear, my polar jacket: to get undressed I didn't even wait for them to turn away. One of them passed me a boiler suit. Then they put a blanket over my back. They were rubbing my hands and feet. Suddenly I realized how frozen I was.

I asked them to close the door of the helicopter; I couldn't stand the sight of the sea any more.

I recall finding myself in a seat, my feet on the co-pilot's thighs, where he was rubbing them. Another man was working on my hands. And I said, "I'm thirsty, I would like to drink something."

And the co-pilot answered that there was nothing but Coke to drink. I burst out laughing. They told me to drink slowly and I obeyed. Then I said, "I'm hungry."

They had nothing to eat, nothing but peanuts. So I ate the peanuts, and my hand was trembling so much that I could hardly get them in my mouth. They were salty, so salty. And I moaned to myself, "Dear God, couldn't I have something else to eat besides this salty stuff?"

They ask me how many we were on the raft, and what had happened.

I mumble an answer. Bernard dead, I don't know what caused it, left to the sea . . . my daughter . . . silence. I could not talk about my daughter.

One of the men understands that I do not feel like talking.

"I lost someone three weeks ago, I know how you are feeling . . . Let's not talk about it. Try to forget . . ."

I could not bring myself to describe in detail the horror of Gaëlla's death, or my reaction. I could already tell that no one would understand. And what would be the point? I thought I would be left alone. I was on land, so the land should welcome me with kindness, tenderness; it should pamper me, warm me, feed me, wash me in fresh water, and love me. That was the least it could do. You have to be a survivor to understand that. To have experienced a tragedy, to have fought with death and learned to live with the death of others.

But those who are waiting for you on land are not necessarily welcoming. The last survivor is guilty of survival. It's strange, but it's as if the land were angry with me for having survived.

I thought of my mother, of our first words. To her I could relate what had happened. Tell her everything. It was no one else's business.

My mistake.

CHAPTER SIX

On Land

O N THE RAFT I had counted only on myself. I
was alone in the world with Gaëlla. Every gesture was important: getting up, sitting down,
watching the sea, bailing, filling the bottle, making
Gaëlla drink, counting the mouthfuls, looking after
her, distracting her, speaking endlessly to keep from
going crazy.

Once I was back on land all my strength gave out.
I said to myself, it's all over, let others take care of
things, at last I have nothing more to do or to decide.

The helicopter landed in La Coruña, Spain, in a
pouring rain.

This disgusting fresh water falling from the sky no
longer means a thing to me. I couldn't care less about
clouds and all that. An ambulance pulls up, with a
stretcher.

"I can walk, you know."

But they force me to lie down. I see curious faces

peering in at me through the glass. The sound of the motor and the siren causes me to make contact with reality once again. It's a bit humiliating to be transported like this, I can't stand to be seen in such a weak state. In fact, even if in my mind I thought I could walk, my legs would never have carried me.

The blanket pulled up to my nose, I arrive at the emergency room of the hospital. A crowd of people are moving all around me; it's terrifying, comforting and exhausting. No one listens when I say:

"I'm hungry . . . I would like to eat. I'm thirsty . . . I would like to drink . . ."

Instead of bringing me the mountain of food I had dreamt of so often for days, they ask me for my blood type, name, date of birth, address, occupation; they tell me not to worry, that I'm in good hands, that everything is fine.

They treat me as if I were sick, talking to me as if I were going to collapse.

I know everything is fine. I am lucid, I'm hungry and thirsty and I would like a shower. I really would! They don't understand; they look at me as if I were dying. After they take my blood, I am hopeful once again, thinking the formalities are over and they will at last give me something to eat.

Here I am in an uncomfortable, rough bed; the plastic cover under the sheet crackles and makes creases; the pillow is lumpy. And here I was dreaming of a big soft, sumptuous bed; I stare at the white ceiling, my eyes wide open, a drip in my arm.

"Rest now."

The doctor went over me from every angle: the whites of my eyes, my tongue, my pulse, my legs, my heart.

"I'm hungry . . ."

"Just relax. You mustn't eat now, your stomach would not stand it."

My bum hurts. The humidity and the salt, the dehydration, the cold, the smell of rubber lingering on my skin—I should have a hot bath. Wash my body, as if it were a baby's; massage it, oil it, dry it, perfume it. I would like to change my smell, change the very stuff I'm made of, and above all, can't someone give me something to eat!

The doctor has left and I begin to beg all the nurses who go past. A cracker, a hot chocolate, some fruit. Give me back my life.

"That wouldn't be a good idea. And anyway, the kitchen is closed."

I am furious. I am not sick! I am dying of hunger and thirst! Can't they understand? Finally one of the nurses succumbs and furtively brings me, as if she had stolen them, a hot chocolate and a bunch of grapes.

She watches me carefully. The first swallow is marvelous. Hot. Sweet—I cannot stop swirling the creamy liquid over my tongue, moving it around my mouth; I am delaying the moment of swallowing this precious thing, my hands are trembling with emotion around the cup as if I had just been given the Eucharist.

I swallow. When you haven't eaten anything for two weeks, an eternity, swallowing is miraculous. I would like to talk, to touch someone, to make sure I am on earth and not dreaming. I swallowed something! The rainwater catchment cone on the raft stank of brackish water, and the taste was dreadful. This fabulous mouthful of hot chocolate cannot be described.

I clasp the nurse's hand: a human being is standing here, next to me. I would like to talk, tell my story to this living person. Talking is as violent a need as hunger and thirst. She has difficulty detaching herself from me. I would cry if I could, but I am not used to tears.

And yet that is what I should do. Cry, break down, go to pieces. For my nerves, first of all, to release them from the awful tension they have been through. And also, so that the others will understand me. These first moments in my hospital room, sipping the hot chocolate, sucking on a grape, slowly but with a terrible urgency, and my need to fill the silence: the nurse does not understand any of this.

She must think I'm a wreck, incapable of eating; I should vomit the hot chocolate. I should be ravaged by suffering, I should be delirious. Instead, I am swallowing, biting on a grape, and I can't stop talking.

She looks at me not as a survivor but almost as if I were a monster. At the time I don't realize this, but my natural physical resistance is going to create problems of understanding between myself and the rest of the wide world.

Survivors of a disaster should be treated differently. Now I know this. A survivor is not just a body in more or less decent shape, to be weighed, examined, taken here or there, without any thought given to what that survivor is saying. A survivor comes back into the world of the living with all his or her past. Not only the past of her life, but also the past of her near death.

You feel like throwing yourself into life, violently. That is the urgency felt by the survivor. In any case, that is the way I felt. So you are, by necessity, different from a usual "patient." You feel like saying:

"It's *me*! Listen to me, speak to me, I am unique!"

As if everyone knew who I am. I need special attention. I don't give a damn about the fact I have hypothermia, 90 degrees is just a soulless number to me, and the word doesn't interest me. I am shivering, that is simple enough, and I already know it. Physically and morally.

A heated blanket, okay, but give me also arms, hands, a face, someone to look at me, and a listening ear. Take me in your arms.

Instead they cart me around like a parcel in a trolley, and I am smothering beneath this damned blanket; I would like to tear it off.

"Just relax, your temperature is very low."

Rinse me off with fresh water, please. Shower me with soap, with suds, give me soft, dry towels. Give me something dry, not something which smothers me!

The first night in this hospital is a nightmare. I am afraid of dying. This first night on land in a hot, dry bed: I spoke so much of it with Gaëlla, we dreamt of it, so much, the two of us.

"The first night we'll sleep together in a good bed with a pile of pillows and cushions, we'll have a good cuddle, and we'll sleep a long time, a very long time, both of us."

She is not here. How it hurts to realize that, in the darkness of this room where I have been ordered to sleep. No one there. There is actually a woman in the next bed, but she is old and speaks Spanish, and besides, she's asleep. I cannot sleep; how can I sleep, if I fall asleep I am going to die. I am alone. There is no one left but me.

I put Gaëlla into the sea. She left on that mass of gray liquid, and here am I, like an imbecile, like a culprit. My eyes hurt, my lids are burning. I am so cold. So afraid.

I wanted to get up earlier, to stand up: it's important to stand when you've spent two weeks squatting down, your back curved, your knees bent. It's as important as drinking and eating. To stand is to be alive. My legs won't hold me. My mind demands that they work, that they hold me up, but they refuse. Nothing but trembling below the waist, an emptiness.

I am doomed to lie down. I cannot scream the way I did on the raft, you can't do that in a hospital room. You can't insult God because he has saved you. You remain silent because there is no one, because everyone else alive has disappeared, their tasks accomplished. I am going to die.

My mother. How are they going to tell her about Gaëlla's death? I don't want anyone to speak to her before I do. I want my mother. That consul who came to take my papers said a freighter, the *Soro*, had located the *Jan Van Gent,* adrift, on October 10. Two days later the sailboat was salvaged.

Bernard had sworn as much to me, just before he died. "They've found the boat, I know they have." And that freighter—that was the phantom vessel that Bernard had seen.

The consul also told me he would notify my family that the search was over. All of a sudden I realized what that meant. My mother and brothers were aware of our disappearance. They must have thought we were dead, all three of us, when they found the empty sailboat. Dead, all three of us. They're going to tell them I'm alive. They're going to wonder. How did Bernard die, of course, but, above all, Gaëlla? I can already hear my mother's voice:

"Where is Gaëlla? What have you done with my granddaughter?"

My mother did not like Bernard. Or my marriage, or even my divorce. She resented him across the board for being who he was: according to her, an unstable adventurer. Already, when I told her we were going to take off with him, she refused to understand. She judged him before the fact, and now fate has proven her right. I absolutely must be the first one to speak to her. And I dread facing her. When the consul asked me whom I wanted to notify, I answered:

"Notify my brother Paul."

To delay the moment, to take my time before facing the most important woman in my life, after Gaëlla. My daughter, my mother. I no longer have my daughter, and I will have to explain that to my mother. Tell her why I did not bring her back with me.

The night is full of bad dreams: seeing Gaëlla again, dancing, whirling in her dress, on the deck, laughing:

"Daddy, look!"

The nightmare of the Russian freighter, killing us instead of saving us. My daughter is gone. I am without her. It is unfair. She should not have died. She should be here asking for hot chocolate and sausages, her Barbie doll and some chewing gum. She had lost weight, but I saw nothing that might have prepared me for her brutal death. What did my daughter die of? Exhaustion? Fear? The fantastic hope which turned to disaster?

She was no longer fighting. She no longer wanted to fight, that last day. And yet I am certain that if that cursed freighter had hoisted us on board she would have survived. But the Russian sailors were courageous, they did everything; it is the murderous ocean which caused her to lose the fight. I know they all cried. It is the sea I hate, not the men. How can I tell my mother about that drowned look on her face, the water on her cheeks, my inability to hold her, dead, in my arms? How? To lower one's child into the sea is not a ceremony she can understand.

In the jumble of images invading my sleeplessness—the wave, the raft, the freighter—I did not realize that at dawn I sank into a restless sleep. My neighbor told me, gently, that morning. I must have had nightmares and I called out to my daughter, incessantly. When I awake, the doctor and nurses begin their exams again.

"Mommy, I want to put my tutu and my tights back on. I am going to do lots of dancing, that way I'll learn to do a cartwheel.

"Mommy, I want to get married."

"Who with, sweetheart?"

"We'll see, it doesn't matter now. I want a baby. I want a long dress with a veil, fifteen feet long, a train, with little flowers on my head and a bouquet in my hand. I love flowers, Mommy, I love shells, I love music, I love making braids with my hair, I love dresses with ruffles, and white shoes. I love socks with lace on them."

She loved life.

"Stand up, Gaëlla, you have to walk, Mommy has to blow up the rings."

"No, Mommy, stay a bit longer, I feel good like this . . ."

"We have to look out for boats."

"I don't care about the boats . . . I don't want to move, I have a tummy ache. Mommy, do you think I'm being punished because I didn't finish my plate? Can Daddy see us? Is he going to help us? Where is Daddy?"

"Daddy is in the clouds, he's sleeping."

I could not pronounce the word, "dead." Nor could I say "corpse," or "body." I need to keep the names of living people. Bernard is asleep somewhere, Daddy is asleep somewhere.

"Can't you tell him to call some nice ladies and gentlemen and tell them to come and get us?"

She was singing *La mère Michel qui a perdu son chat* and *Il court il court le furet*.

Everyone thought she had been carried off by a wave. I can only tell the truth to my mother, because she will demand to know. My daughter's disappearance is too personal a thing for me to give it to other people, to strangers in my life.

My roommate has had a visit from her daughter. Yesterday that young woman asked me gently in French if there was anything I would like. Flowers, I answered. To touch life.

"My name is Marie. If you need anything else, don't hesitate to ask. Will your family be coming?"

"My brother Paul and his wife, Chantal."

"There's a crowd of reporters outside."

The nurses are muttering about intruders trying to take photos through the windows. I need clothes, a toothbrush and some toothpaste. I have nothing left on earth. Yesterday was Thursday. October 20.

I stayed six days in the hospital. The scramble began on Friday evening.

Paul and Chantal did not know what to say to the journalists. Neither did I. The consul wanted me to leave with my brother, in his car; this whole business was creating problems for him. He wanted money for everything; all I wanted was a toothbrush and to be left alone. I had to beg for three days before Marie was able to bring me what I needed to have a clean mouth again. The consul only saw things in the light of his red tape: the burden of the hospital for a survivor who was costing a lot of money.

"There will be an inquest, that's normal. I have to know the circumstances in which your husband disappeared. And your daughter as well. The captain of the freighter filed a report and I have to compare your statement with his."

I had to tell him the truth. It wasn't a wave, it was me.

That consul got on my nerves. I wanted to phone my mother, talk to her; I was eager to unburden my story. But the phone didn't work, or I was supposed to wait for who knows what. The consul's own portable telephone was not working either, or so he said.

Maybe I thought someone was going to bring me a phone in my bed? Did I think I was at the Ritz? You can't call France just like that, from the phone booth of a Spanish hospital . . .

I finally got through to my mother on Tuesday, the sixth day. In the meanwhile my brother had given the reporters the bare bones of the story: the storm, how we left the sailboat, Bernard's death, how I had to put his body into the ocean after three days, then the two of us, hanging on, the Russian freighter, and Gaëlla carried off by a wave. He had repeated the official version.

But the consul, to whom I had been more or less obliged to give an unofficial version of the last hours after the aborted rescue attempt, thought nothing of giving my story to the media, to a Spanish magazine of his choice, *El Mundo*. Nor did he hesitate for an instant to let them use our passport photos. He wanted to get rid of me, and also of the reporters. The hospital was surrounded, I was creating a disturbance, I would do better to go to a hotel or leave by car with my brother. With what? What money? In what state? I was incapable of walking for more than ten minutes, but my healthy looks seemed to imply the contrary.

And there was I, who had naively believed that land was waiting for me, that it would take me in its arms and smile to me. Now it's cross with me, suspicious, making assumptions, and, above all, talking about money. That is all that land is interested in. Money for the consul, money for the salvage of the *Jan Van Gent*, money for the helicopter. The reporters' money. Give the dogs a bone to gnaw on and they'll do the rest.

There will have to be a press conference. The consul thinks that is the best solution, so that the hospital can have some peace again. These people are fed up with having this Louise Longo person between their walls, this Frenchwoman who put her husband into the sea, who lost her daughter, and whom no one has had a chance to interview. She owes it to the reporters. There are the Spanish and French television channels and representatives of the press agencies and magazines.

They sat me down in a wheel chair, like an invalid, and pushed me in front of this curtain of camera crews and photographers. And at that moment I thought about my mother. Her first vision of me, alive, after all that anxiety, and the reporters were going to spread it around all over the place. So I smiled. To show her I was all right. If we had been alone together, my mother and I, I would have given her the same smile. I did not imagine at that moment that my smile was going to bother everyone. That my inability to say to them, "I put my daughter into the sea . . ." was going to turn me into a culprit.

They told me there would be an inquest and that I would have to answer certain questions for a judge. I thought I would be meeting him. There was no judge. There were reporters who wanted their copy, and television people asking all sorts of stupid questions:

"How did you feel as you were putting your husband's body into the water? How did you feel when Gaëlla died? Did you suffer from hunger? Why did you leave the sailboat? Why was it found almost intact? You don't seem to have suffered too much physically. Did you really go fifteen days without eating?"

You can't answer questions like this in one sentence, in a few words, in a hurry beneath the flashing of cameras. I'm no movie star used to controlling my answers. I said almost nothing. And with that nothing they did what they pleased.

I only saw the judge after the press conference.

A French magazine, with a by-line by a charming woman, displayed this vitriolic title: "The next day, she was smiling."

"There were three of them, and today she has no husband, no daughter . . . and this disturbing smile. Shock? Anti-depressants? Surely. But, as a rule, widowhood dresses elegantly, in more somber tones . . . and in this case, well, what is one to think . . . no one feels like consoling a laughing widow . . ."

I am now in the category of the "merry widows." They compare me to Betty Maxwell, the wife of the famous press magnate who disappeared into the drink and was never seen again.

I don't understand. It hurts. It hurts even more that a woman is being so gratuitously aggressive with me. What right has she to be so high-minded? Why should I justify my suffering according to some established norms? Why do they think they can judge my entire life in just a few lines, on the basis of a survivor's smile? Should I, from the start, have said to the photographers:

"Tell them that is just how Louise Longo is, that she needs to smile to her mother, above all. Print, in the headlines, that Louise Longo has always stood up to adversity and misfortune, and thanks her stars to be alive. Tell them, too, that suffering is not necessarily visible on a face, that the ruin of a body and soul can be interior, secret, invisible on a roll of film. Tell them that I ask the entire world to forgive me for being alive. Excuse me for not having died, or at least gone mad, where I could be safe from your stupid interrogations."

Marie, very quickly, became a friend. I can be with her husband Jose and her daughter Eva and feel a part of their family, one of them. Today they are my new family. The one I have chosen. She took me home, supported me, fed me, listened to me, forgave me. I stayed there for three weeks, slowly making steps. All through those days she was my mother, my friend, my sister. She gave me her time and her love, she restored my faith and self-confidence. Without pity. Just love. The only thing that did not work in my survivor's body was walking. I didn't really understand why, unless it was because I had been squatting for fifteen days. Later, I was told about iron and magnesium deficiencies, so they gave me some tablets and gradually my legs began to move and keep me standing for more than ten minutes.

I was barely on my feet, wobbly, convalescing in France with my family, when a new accusation came to knock me down again. Marie called me one day from Spain:

"The newspapers are full of accusations. Bernard had not paid for the boat. There will be an investigation in France, and the reporters are saying that the French police are looking for you. They say that there are things about your adventure that don't seem right, that you might have killed your husband and voluntarily put your daughter into the sea. They say no one knows where you are!"

They wrote: *A French judge is searching for the sole survivor of the* Jan Van Gent, *who has disappeared.*

Basically, after disappearing at sea I have disappeared on land? Am I trying to run away?

All these accusations appeared on the front page of the maritime news in La Coruña's papers. The refutations Marie helps me to send to editors do not make the headlines. The press still doubt, therefore, so does the public. The suspicions voiced on Louise Longo's account are of a financial nature. The yacht on which she set sail with her husband and daughter had not been paid for.

I feel soiled, humiliated. I want to know where the accusation has come from, and I am told it was from a newspaper in southwestern France. I call for a whole week without getting hold of anyone who will answer my questions. The wrong has been done, but everyone is away on winter break! I finally call the police station; the same result. At last, long after January 1, a policeman answers:

"But they're not looking for you! If they were, they would have found you already a long time ago!"

That is how I learned the truth about Bernard and the *Jan Van Gent*. He had not paid for the boat. He had taken us on board, his daughter and me, and he knew all along. And as the sole survivor, what else could I be but an accomplice?

In May 1995, I underwent a detailed interrogation. I had not been living with Bernard for two years, we had only gotten back together for Gaëlla's sake. Once again I had to justify myself to them. Just as I had to justify my appetite for life. Because I had not said to the reporters:

"You know, I was afraid of dying at the hospital, I was afraid I would just be cleaned out, lose my guts, my eyes were hurting and they still hurt me. I couldn't walk or hold anything in my hands without trembling. I was deficient in calcium, magnesium and iron; I had a rash all over my bum—do you want to see it?" And also: "I have no permanent residence, no work, I pay no taxes in France, I did odd jobs off the books in the West Indies, in order to raise my daughter. And take note of the fact that I left my husband because he had begun drinking and was depressive. Do you want me to tell you the violence in detail? Do you want to know the day and the time he raised his hand against me? At what point I told him, 'Ciao, you go your way, I'll go mine.'"

And this too, above all: "You know, a man is a complicated thing. He was a father at the age of twenty, and he didn't assume his role, but when he turned fifty he began to cling to a little five-year-old girl. And the little girl, who knew nothing about her father's life, who didn't care what it was, well, she loved him, she wanted to be with him! He wasn't a monster and I did not feel I had the right to stop her seeing her father. When you've loved for a long time, you don't just start hating to that degree! You want me to explain friendship to you?"

I ask for respect for him; he's no longer here to defend himself. Only I have the right to say he was not perfect, that he had his weaknesses, and that he died as he lived, an adventurer. He was my daughter's father, that is the only thing that matters.

I agreed to tell my story to *Paris-Match*, because the reporter who suggested it was the only one who was understanding. And the money I received for the article allowed me to survive. That's it, yes, survive, and I'm still surviving! Allowed me to eat, to find a bed to sleep in, without taking refuge in other people's homes. But in order to toss a bouquet of flowers into the sea, in memory of my daughter, I had to hide, so that the reporters would not track me down.

At the hospital I had asked for a priest. I wanted him to say a benediction for her. All they said was:

"A priest? You want to make confession?"

I also fought for my story to appear in its entirety in a specialized magazine, *Voiles et Voiliers*.[1] Written by a sailor, who knows what he's talking about. So that our tragic experience might serve as a positive lesson to others, so that they might learn to double-check their liferafts, and not just at the last minute.

In the end, in order to unburden myself definitively of the weight of my story, I decided to meet a publisher. In the midst of all these accusations, I had the feeling I had never really told my story to anyone. That I hadn't had time to tell it to a patient listener, who would not judge me *a priori*, but would simply accept my tale. For sure, I can already hear the voices of the specialists, the psychologists, saying:

"Well why don't you go into therapy? Why not a psychiatrist instead of a book? That's indecent, a book; it will sell!"

At the risk of shocking, which no longer matters to me whatsoever, I will reply that you pay for the couch, in any case. Whereas the tape recorder which has taken down my words is something I can afford, psychologically and financially. I refuse to sit and cry

---

[1] French equivalent to *Sail* or *Cruising World*.

in front of a psychiatrist. I refuse to cry, period, to give in to the lure of the sad, sordid sides of life.

I have lost everything. I had only my daughter, she was more to me than all the bank accounts on earth. I am ruined by her disappearance, that's true. I am guilty in the eyes of my mother because I did not return with her so tiny, solid, fragile body in my arms. But that is a private conflict, between the two of us. It is easier for me to bear, not having a grave to visit. I do not belong to those survivors who need to cry over a stone, or a commemorative plaque, an eternal monument to memory. I preserve the image of Gaëlla as she was, living; her smile does not frighten me. She sleeps, in the sea.

I am one of those survivors who refuse sorrow. What good would it do to cry for the rest of my life? Logic—my own, that is—dictates that you should commit suicide in such a case. For me, you don't go shouting, "I will die of sorrow" unless you intend to do it.

I almost killed myself in the raft; I was in shock. Fate decided otherwise. At the first sign of life in the sky, I lifted my head. I reached out, gratefully, and thanked the land for calling me back.

And so I am a survivor for life. That is my answer. I am alive, I have been allowed to live; for how much longer, I don't know, but during that time I want to see flowers, beauty, I want to have another child, I want to love again. I want to be a mother until I die.

Now that my story has been told, once and for all, I have been set free. Without hate, without remorse, without guilt; I am simply going to go on living, with the experience of my tragedy as additional baggage. I love having a future ahead of me. I love seeing the sun rise, even above the sea; I love life, a slice of bread, rain, a strolling passerby, a new dress, the smile of a friend. I love each coming day, even before it arrives. More than ever.

As for living, I hope to do it somewhere where no one knows me, where no one will ask questions about the past, unless I can freely, of my own will, confide what I choose to confide.

As for living, it is the only thing which matters, for as long as one is alive.

Paris, August 1995.

THE ODYSSEY OF THE JAN VAN GENT

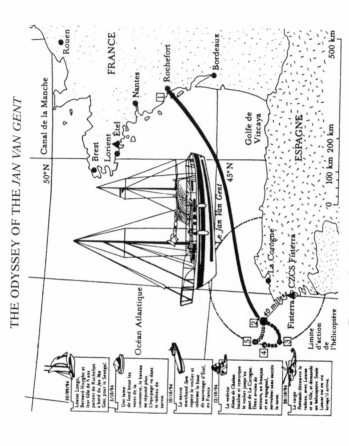

Drawing by Xoán G. *La Voz de Galicia*

Other titles of interest

The Captain's Guide to Liferaft Survival
by Michael Cargal

Everything a castaway needs to know to survive in a liferaft and get rescued as quickly as possible. It contains essential information on choosing and equipping a liferaft, food and water, medical care, rescue procedures and more.

117 Days Adrift
by Maurice and Maralyn Bailey

When their yacht was hit and sunk by a whale, the Bailey family was destined to enter the record books. Their survival for nearly four months in a rubber raft is a fantastic human story of adaptation to totally alien conditions.

Survive the Savage Sea
by Dougal Robertson

"For stark excitement, marine natural history, practical lessons, and human love and stresses, few records, if any, of hazard and survival have ever bettered it." *Washington Post*

Desperate Voyage
by John Caldwell

To be reunited with his new bride, the author and his kittens face sharks, shipwrecks, starvation and a hurricane aboard the 29-foot *Pagan*. An unforgettable adventure.

Tamata and the Alliance
by Bernard Moitessier

This internationally acclaimed biography spans Moitessier's life from early childhood in Indochina until the months before his death. It is a fascinating book of spiritual growth and high adventure.

Sheridan House
America's Favorite Sailing Books